D1176698

ACKNOWLEDGMENTS

A common need of writers when struggling to finish their project is encouragement. And thankfully many of my friends bolstered my spirits by generously providing me their on-going support.

Chase's memoir would not have been completed without the aid of my critique group. They provided numerous suggestions by reviewing page after page of my writing. Mary Ann Clark, Dawn Baertlein, Marian Powell, and Jeanne Mackenzie have my sincerest gratitude.

Special thanks to Paul Moret, Liv Weiss, Kathy Polvino, Susy Jenkins, and Hanya Gonzales who read early drafts of the Chase manuscript and were keen in spotting errors and inconsistencies.

Heidi Thomas, an award-winning author, not only did a marvelous job of editing my manuscript but was also generous with recommendations for helping me improve my writing.

I sincerely appreciate the willingness, time and effort from all.

To Marianne

Chase loved you as much as you loved him.

OTHER BOOKS BY RICHARD BOICH

The Immaculate Deception – A Thriller

The Epitome of Greed and Evil – A Mystery

A TRIBUTE TO ALL DOGS

"The one absolutely unselfish friend that man can have in this selfish world, the one that never deserts him, the one that never proves ungrateful or treacherous, is his dog. A man's dog stands by him in prosperity and in poverty, in health and in sickness. He will sleep on the cold ground, where the wintry winds blow and the snow drives fiercely, if only he may be near his master's side. He will kiss the hand that has no food to offer, he will lick the wounds and sores that come in encounter with the roughness of the world. He guards the sleep of the pauper master as if he were a prince. When all other friends desert, he remains. When riches take wings and reputation falls to pieces, he is as constant in his love as the sun in its journey through the heavens."

Senator George Vest, 1870

TABLE OF CONTENTS

CHAPTER

1

ME

Hi, my name is Chase, and I have a tail to tell. I guess to be grammatically correct, I should say a tale. I don't want to make a bad impression to start my story.

I'm a Rhodesian Ridgeback. I think. Doubt creeps in because the critics who challenge my breeding say that I have too many physical imperfections. They say my tail is too fat, my coat is too coarse and golden in color, and I'm just too broad chested. So, I don't meet the official Rhodesian Ridgeback standards, and I'm a fraud if I make the claim to be one.

My human mom, also referring to the standards would say that the small ridge along my back, my muscular shoulders, a dignified, quiet temperament that includes being protective and affectionate of loved ones, qualifies me. And that's why she deemed me a Ridgeback. So, who do you believe? My beloved mom or a bunch of people who may not know the difference between a dog and a cat? Regardless, I like the Rhodesian Ridgeback label and am proud to wear it.

The Ridgeback is from Africa, and we were bred to hunt large animals. Often lions. Yeah, the king of the jungle. You might ask, if the lion was king—some say the meanest, toughest predator in the jungle, five times our size—why were we hounding him?

Well, our breed's modus operandi for hunting the king would start with a pack of five or six of us. We all weighed about 85 pounds and our raised hackles made us look larger. Plus, we are fast and very athletic. When confronting the brut we would dart in and out at his flank and rump to confuse him until the hunter arrived. That's how we performed our role.

Officially though, I'm probably a mutt even though my human Mom and Dad never called me that. However I didn't care about my heritage as long as I got fed regularly, and I did.

Now I'm about ten years old and live with my family of humans and canine friends in a rural area of Medford, Oregon. My birthplace was in Phoenix, Arizona and I'll tell you how we got to Oregon shortly. But first I'll explain how the idea of my memoir began.

My dad and I were sitting on a bale of hay in the barn while he sipped a cup of his morning coffee. He glanced at me. "You've had a lifetime of interesting experiences." He took another sip and then draped an arm around my shoulder. "You should share your adventures with others." I glanced at him and noticed the gray stubble on his face. He hadn't shaved this morning. "Write a book. I can help you."

I ignored him.

The next morning we walked the front pasture's fence line checking for needed repairs. He swore a few times as he found holes where the wire needed mending. At one point he patted my head and repeated his book idea. "You've had a lot of funny, sad, and exciting episodes that others would enjoy reading. And they would appreciate your intelligence and wit."

Dad stumbled to one knee. "Damn gopher holes." He stood, brushed his pant leg, and continued his questioning, "What about it? It could be a lot of fun. For both of us."

I understood the human language as do most canines, but we have selective hearing like many children and spouses that I've observed. We pick and choose what we want to hear and act accordingly.

However, Dad and I had this special thing where we could communicate with each other. Yeah, I'd kind of think something, and as if he could read my mind, he would respond. And like I mentioned, I understood what he said to me.

We completed the inspection of the front fence and headed back toward the barn to check the eastside fencing. I thought about his proposal. Having my picture on a book cover for cute lady Ridgebacks to see wasn't a bad idea. Maybe thousands of sweeties from other breeds as well. No romantic relationships though, as I was neutered long ago. But maybe to share a hamburger under the stars and start a friendship.

"Okay," I told him. "But I don't know the names for some things and can't spell anyhow, so you have to do all the writing."

"Yeah," he snickered, "And I remember how you tried to paw a Valentine's Day note to Mom on my computer keyboard."

I remembered too. My effort to write a poem looked like it was written in Greek or Russian.

Dad dropped to a knee and hugged me. "Sounds like we have a deal." To us, the embrace meant we had a contract signed in blood.

So through Dad, I'll be sharing memories of my human and canine family as best I can recall them. Then you decide how interesting my life has been.

"Dogs do speak, but only to those who listen."

Orhan Pamuk

CHAPTER

2

THE EXPERIMENT

Have you ever been in the spotlight? The focus of an experiment with hundreds of creatures depending on you for survival? That's how it all began with me.

The original idea for Mom when she fostered me from the Arizona Humane Society didn't work out as planned. So before I explain what happened, I'll give a little background. Dad was a member of the Humane Society's board of directors, and he, along with many others, were concerned about the millions of dogs and cats who were euthanized every year. Yeah, holocaust-like. My friends. Probably some of my relatives too.

There were too many creatures and no place for them to live.

Note: *Today, two decades later, the national pet overpopulation issue continues but thankfully at a lesser degree. Greater awareness by people to spay and neuter their pets, and more animal shelters that practice a no-kill philosophy have led to the decline in deaths.*

Well-intentioned people too often contribute to the dispatch of animals. They are good people who adopt with the best of intentions. However they aren't always well-informed on how to absorb their new canine family member into a human household. And as a result some of my peers are given a deadly label of "Bad dog." They are not bad, but poorly trained or not trained at all. But because of that undeserved characterization, many are added to the euthanasia statistics.

A news flash! We're cute and cuddly, but we are not humans. And we won't understand your way of living on the first day we enter your house. Yes, people get frustrated and angry when canines chew, dig, and pee in the wrong places. But digging and chewing are in our genes. Peeing and pooping are natural to all creatures. And I assure you that "attitude adjustment" spankings will make matters worse. We're smart enough to negotiate a deal. Give us some guidance and consistency, and in a few days, we'll get with the program.

Professional dog trainers are available in most communities so please bring us to one. And after the training, both the human and canine will better understand how to create a loving, lifetime relationship.

Okay, no more preaching, and on to my story.

My foster mom Marianne, and her business partner Joann, ran a puppy training school called the *Sunshine School for Dogs.* Yeah, a school where dogs learned proper etiquette and how to make friends and influence humans. The training philosophy was based on positive reinforcement and rewards. And never striking or shouting in anger at your pet.

"When living in a human home, do as the humans do." I think Shakespeare or maybe St. Ambrose said something like that. So, canines should follow the house rules, and Mom and Joann promoted that attitude to their canines and human students

Dog handlers were given basic, but sometime overlooked, "tips for the arrival of a "new child." For example, how to prepare your dogs' sleeping arrangements, the type and amounts of food they should eat, and surprising to some, the need to manage small children around their new friends. Their program included discussions about regular medical checkups, ID chips to help identify lost dogs, and the advantages of knowing the history and expectations of your dog's breeding. The big thing? How to teach the new family member where to poop and pee.

The physical training included how to walk at their master's side without pulling, and when, on command, to sit, stay, come, and lie down.

Overall I think Mom and Joann must have recommended a thousand details to the dog handlers.

So, here's the point. Mom would foster a pup from the Humane Society and then train the critter at her school. After completing the training, she would return the graduate to the shelter for adoption. The idea, of course, was that the education would improve the dog's odds to succeed in a human household. And obviously, I was the pup she selected for the training.

Mom and Dad hoped that the training model would be shared with others. What if every obedience club, rescue group, agility club or professional dog trainer would foster and educate two or three puppies a year? It would result in more happy endings and fewer sad deaths of so-called incorrigible canines.

"The greatness of a nation and its moral progress can be judged by the way its animals are treated."

Mahatma Gandhi

CHAPTER

3

THE CHOSEN ONE

Do you know the date of your birth? I'm not sure of mine. The folks at the Arizona Humane Society (AHS) said that I entered the world in Phoenix in early July. Believe me, summer in that city is not a good time for a canine to be born. I think I learned to pant before I learned to breathe. The first thing I remember was that it felt like being inside a volcano. Then, a fog hovered over me and when the murkiness cleared, I found myself caged at the Humane Society. Why? I'm just a puppy. I'm not a criminal. Do humans put their babies in cages too?

I was in rows of kennels with scores of compatriots, barking and whining. Some huddled in the corners of their cages, terrified by all the racket. I had been interned at the shelter for only a few days, but I already knew the routine. A human face entering our kennel meant possible adoption. And we all wanted to be pardoned from what we considered being unfair imprisonment.

Then, in August, a woman from the AHS staff walked into our kennel with a lady we had not seen before. Sensing that the lady was here to adopt one of us, we began showcasing our attention-grabbing techniques.

Some dogs unsure how to behave, flashed their fangs. The frantic vaulted against their chain link walls creating sounds like an orchestra of poorly tuned cellos. Others presented a calmer routine and just sat at their door and wagged their tails. I wanted to look the ladies in the eye so with my paws high on the cage wall, I waited for them to walk my way.

Usually, the place smelled like a hospital, and the scent of the antiseptic cleaning liquids burned my muzzle. But when the Chow in cage three got excited, she would poop and float a stinky, invisible cloud that would hang about two feet above the floor. And now she was all shook up.

Would the smell that drifted like mustard gas in the World War I trenches stampede the humans? And my chance for a new home?

Undaunted by the odor the women peered into the cages as they sauntered closer to me. They stopped at the cage next to mine, which held a young, black mixed breed. "He's exactly what I had in mind," said the lady.

"I'd reconsider," I heard the staff person reply. "When the dog is trained, we'll arrange PR time with a local television station. His dark color won't show well on TV." And she went on to say, "Some people don't like black dogs and won't adopt them."

The new lady frowned.

Now, the two women stopped in front of cage number 13. Mine. "Isn't he sweet?" The lady's eyes were warm and friendly, yet sad. I could tell she wanted to take all of us home with her.

Sunlight peeked from one of the windows behind my row of cages and made her auburn hair glow. I could also see that her eyes were brown. Like mine. So we at least had something in common. I hoped it would be enough for her to pick me.

The staff woman opened the cage and snapped a leash to my collar, and the three of us headed outside to the play area. The new lady firmly held my leash while I attempted to show my friendliness by licking her face. Crude maybe, but you only get one chance to make a good first impression.

"Okay, little guy," she said. "Calm down."

I did. She watched my demeanor and spoke to me to me in a soft voice as we walked around the area. I tried to act cool, but I was so excited I almost peed on her shoes.

Bottom line, she chose me. Picked, in part, because my coat wasn't black. It's weird that some humans select their friends because of color.

I already mentioned Dad was a member of the Arizona Humane Society Board of Directors. I'm not sure what being a board meant other than to build dog houses. But he had arranged for Mom to present her training idea to the AHS management staff, and thankfully the Education Director approved the puppy-fostering plan. That's how I was chosen for the program.

**"If there are no dogs in Heaven, then when I die
I want to go where they went."**

Will Rogers

CHAPTER

4

MY TEMPORARY HOME

I had been given an opportunity, and now I had to make the humans understand how much I wanted to belong.

Gazing out the car window as we left the shelter's parking lot, I had feelings of freedom and joy, but also sadness. Sadness for my peers still behind those walls, locked in their cages and waiting to be part of a loving, human home. And also heartbroken for those who would depart in a black plastic bag because there was no more room.

My foster Mom stopped at a traffic light and I caught sight of a young, terrified German Shepherd bounding through the intersection. Car brakes squealed as the dog ran to a man standing at the bus stop. The man turned his back. Rejected, the shepherd darted back across the street. Brakes screeched again. I followed his flight of fear until he disappeared in a small strip mall, undoubtedly searching for someone who would welcome the loyalty I knew he would give.

When we pulled into the driveway of my new home, I saw lush green grass for the first time in my life. I jumped out of the car and ran in crazy, wild circles inside the low, stuccoed wall that lined the lawn. Two towering cottonwood trees stood like sentinels as they shaded the front of the house.

Foster Mom opened a gate and led me into the backyard. A tall cedar fence bordered the grassy area and a majestic fan palm tree stood in the far corner. After I had taken no more than five steps, two Shetland Sheepdogs arrived on the scene and yapped at me. Mom introduced me. Diamond, apparently the daughter of the two, nipped at my butt, treating me like a squirrel. Man, I was almost ready to sprint back to the shelter.

Diamond was about nine years old and gorgeous. She wore a golden coat with a snow-white bib that dominated her breast. Her mother, Dancer, who was smaller, stood about fourteen inches tall at the shoulder. She had toffee-colored fur, with a creamy white collar and patches of butterscotch on her snout and legs.

Alerted by the commotion, Geoff, a young Border Collie, appeared. He was dressed in a black and white coat. I later found out that he had arrived in the household just weeks earlier. He was a permanent family member but destined for a different type of training. I'll get to his story a little later in my tale.

Mom knelt beside me. "Chase, You'll meet Laura, our daughter, when she gets home from high school. She's very pretty, and she loves dogs."

She talked to me as if I was a human. It was the first time anyone had treated me like that. Wow! Is this what life as part of a human family meant?

The Shelties had some formal names as if they were from some Scottish royalty or maybe related to the King of England. Dancer's birth pedigree name? Bilgowan Dancing Allegro. It fit her, always waltzing around as if dancing to Johann Strauss's music. I learned about classical music from the times I sat at Mom's feet while she listened to that stuff.

Allegro Molto Brillante was Diamond's moniker. Do you know how Webster defines allegro? "A brisk lively tempo." And that name fit her too. She must have had the most active mouth west of the Mississippi River. I thought Diamond should have been named Trumpet or Trombone.

Note-*Shetland Sheepdogs are a vocal breed known for their loud, piercing barks. It is an instinct they use to help herd sheep.*

So, what's in a name? What's yours? I bet it's not Dash or Sprint or Run.

Mom chose my name before Foster Dad even had a say. I remember the look on his face when she told him.

"I don't care what he chased. What are you going to name him?"

Mom told him three times before he got it. But I thought like Dad. Webster says "chase" is commonly used as a verb. A verb expresses what someone or something does–like a canine will *chase* a feline. She was a technical writer and exposed me to the dictionary and how to use it. The book has a lot of dog-eared pages to prove it.

If I may digress for a moment–I can live with the English language, but for the record, canine messaging is the superior form of communication. You growl, raise your hackles, show your fangs or, if necessary, bite a leg. Humans instantly get the memo. No misunderstanding, no ambiguity.

Mom said, "The name Chase sounds aristocratic and dignified.

And chasing is something the little guy will do." She was right. Somewhat. I don't chase tornados, cars, or alligators. But I'd still rather have a more common name and not some labor-intensive verb.

I would have felt better if she'd named me after some famous person. Like Salmon Portland Chase? He was the Secretary of the Treasury and then Chief Justice of the Supreme Court for President Lincoln. Or how about a name like Humphrey? Or Bogie? Didn't he win an Oscar with the movie *The African Queen,* filmed near my ancestral birthplace?

I guess I should be thankful though. Mom could have named me after a river like the Chattahoochee.

"Life is as dear to a mute creature as it is to man.
Just as one wants happiness and fears pain,
just as one wants to live and not die,
so do other creatures."

His Holiness the Dalai Lama

CHAPTER

5

TRAINING TIME

I met Laura, blue eyed and blond, and she was sweet to me. But being a typical teenager, she spent little time with the household canines. I'd get a quick hug from her, and then she'd dash off to meet her friends.

I had become comfortable with my foster family because they all treated me so well—except for the Shelties. But I had accepted the ladies as my canine bosses, and being subservient to them was better than existing at the shelter. I could tell that Dad liked me a lot because the way people talk to you sends a strong signal, and his sounded loud and clear.

I looked to Geoff as my mentor because, unlike the Shelties, he didn't give a howl about canine hierarchy. But he always wanted to chase something, anything, even the broom while Mom swept the floor. One of the first things he taught me was how to get Mom and Dad to respond to his requests. It's called persistence. He'd follow one of them with a toy in his mouth, and whenever they paused he'd drop it at their feet. And he'd continue until they gave in and tossed it. Even in the house.

When outside, chasing a tennis ball was his favorite thing. Fine.

But running after it until he panted like a steam engine seemed crazy to me. Mom's reasoning? He's a Border Collie practicing his herding skills.

But my future was still murky because of my fostered status. And to be a survivor in a human household I knew I had to learn everything I could at puppy school.

The classes were to be held in our back yard, and I know Mom wanted me to be the star student, maybe Phi Beta Kappa, or class valedictorian. After all, that's why I was there–to get an education. Dad would be my handler, and since I would also be the demonstrator, we practiced a lot before the first day of school. Mom and Dad tried to make it playful, yet the heel, sit, stand and stay routines weren't what I call big fun.

Not all my training related to the school. On the west side of the house sat a kidney-shaped swimming pool enclosed by a wrought-iron fence. Of all our backyard activities, Geoff and I enjoyed the water sports the best.

Mom and Dad knew I could swim, but they were concerned about me knowing how to get out of the pool in case of an emergency. Dad held me in his arms the first time we slid into the water. Then Mom called me while she knelt at the head of the steps and showed me where to get out.

But Dad was adamant about water safety. And even though I proved to him that I knew where the steps were after the second demonstration, we probably practiced the routine a hundred times. What I really wanted was to sunbathe on his yellow air mattress, but he never let me try that.

I liked to swim a few laps and then lie on the pool's top steps to cool off. That's the way to beat the Phoenix heat. The only thing missing was a cool glass of beef broth.

The girls knew how to swim but weren't about to get their hair wet. You should have seen their faces when Mom or Dad took them into the water. They resisted as if a shark lurked in the pool, waiting for them.

Rescuing a tennis ball from the pool became Geoff's favorite summer sport. Mom or Dad would toss it into the water, and his belly flop to retrieve it would create a tsunami. He'd hurry up the steps, return the ball, and beg to have it thrown again. And again. Maybe a million times. Crazy. I thought Geoff had lost a slice of bacon from his sandwich. And I wondered if Dad had to refill the pool after Geoff's playtime.

While he played in the water the Shelties would circle the pool and yap. Very annoying. I guess he was having too much fun. Their barking could drown out the roar of a motorcycle.

***

Then the first day of class! Ten students of different breeds, sizes and colors, more excited to play than going to school. Because of all my pre-class homework, I was the top student. However, it became boring for me because of all the repetitions we did to help the struggling puppies. But I must add, they struggled because their human handlers couldn't do their part correctly.

But then during the second week's class session, I spotted an opportunity–a chink in the humans' self-proclaimed superiority over canines. However, if I had thought it through, I wouldn't have acted so obstinate. It could have been a serious black mark on my report card.

One exercise called for Dad and the other handlers to place us in a line and give us a sit-stay command. Then they walked a few steps and turned to face us. The humans stood like tin soldiers, and we were to sit still until called. If we played Statue of Liberty for 30 seconds and returned to our handler's side when beckoned, we were rewarded with a yummy treat.

But if I "absent mindedly" drifted off to smell the flowers, Dad would call me, and I then hustled to his side. Since I obeyed his "come" command, I received a goody. But I still had to repeat the 30-second sit-stay exercise–and when I correctly completed it, I received another treat.

Bottom line, I got two treats while the others received one. I'll let you figure out who got the best of that exercise routine.

Joann was a lot like Mom, and they offered the training because they loved dogs and wanted to help humans better understand us. I'm not comparing them to Mother Teresa, but they sincerely tried to educate dog owners so our lives would be happier. Puppy school turned out to be an hour of fun, especially when a session ended. The canines played while the moms and dads sat around drinking soft drinks and telling stories about us. I made a lot of friends and met some of them at the park from time to time. We would compare notes as to how well our humans were behaving.

When the eight-week training school finished, I received my graduation certificate. I think Dad called it a Canine Associate Degree. And check the acronym. Not funny. Okay. Whatever. But I wondered if Dancer and Diamond, of the Shelty barking breed had previously earned some kind of an advanced degree, like a MOM: Master Of Mouths. They were the experts.

Mom and Joann also taught an agility sport for more mature dogs where you direct your canine through a pre-set obstacle course. Obstacles can include going through tunnels, weave poles, high and broad jumps, and teeter-totters. The routines help build canine confidence. I'll say a bit more about my agility experiences later.

But after graduation, per the plan, I was to be handed like a sweaty baton back to the Humane Society. And from there adopted into a new loving family. Scary, I must admit.

"Heaven goes by favour. If it went by merit, you would stay out and your dog would go in."

Mark Twain

CHAPTER

6

NEAR DEATH

Mom wanted me to be more socialized before I headed back to the Humane Society. So she took me to the park and not only introduced me to every man, woman, and child we met, but it seemed like every tree and rock as well. She made sure I was comfortable in the presence of any animal, vegetable, or mineral.

I appreciated her effort to socialize me, but I had strong personal feelings about Mom and Dad. Positive feelings. Maybe humans would call it love. I had struck gold with them and couldn't imagine being as happy in any other home.

Before Mom fostered me, she had planned to attend a canine instructor's camp in Stockton, California. And now she decided to take me along. Mom thought the traveling experience and meeting new dogs and people would enhance my social skills.

While at the camp, I participated in the obedience class and showed my stuff. I think Mom popped a few buttons because of my performances. The lady who ran the camp told her, "I would keep this one if I were you. He's special. But I've been watching him move, and he has a weak rear. He might fall apart on you."

I didn't know whether to be insulted or not, or what all that meant at the time, but it's another piece of my story.

A few days later when we got home, I didn't feel like eating. For Mom it was bigger news than aliens landing on the White House lawn. But my stomach hurt as if it had been used as a soccer ball, and to escape my pain, I would have gladly spent a week chained to Diamond.

Then Mom discovered that I had a high fever.

The veterinarian at the Humane Society clinic poked me with some torture tools before he announced I had a disease named parvo. (Parvo is a contagious virus mainly affecting dogs and is spread by direct contact with dog feces.) He said I was a sick boy and gave Mom some pills for me to take.

After several days my fever had gone, and my strength started to returned. But in a few days I started suffering terrible bouts of vomiting, Mom rushed me to the animal hospital emergency room and the vet said I now had Corona. (Canine corona is an infectious canine intestinal disease, not the same as COVID-19 virus and not contagious to humans. It is usually short-lived but can be fatal to young dogs.) His eyes became moist as he said, "It's bad." Mom sobbed. Tears gushed.

I spent the night at the hospital and felt better when I woke up the following morning. Better meant strong enough to lift my head and swallow water. The next thing I remember was being at home with Mom cradling me in her arms. Opening my eyes, I spotted a long needle jammed into my front leg and wrapped with white tape. A thin plastic tube led from the needle to a bag of clear liquid that hung from the back of her chair.

Mom sang a lullaby as she encouraged me to sleep. I remember waking up several times, and each time she was still holding me.

The second day Mom placed me into my bed, but I remained hooked up. When Dad came home from work, he asked Mom a lot of questions about me. Then he knelt beside me and stroked my head. I drifted in and out of sleep but remember them agreeing that "He's not going anywhere. He's ours." I didn't get it all they said before I drifted off again.

I slept restlessly for several days, and Mom recognized that my condition had not improved. She shuttled me to a specialist, the third vet since I first got sick. He sent me home with new instructions about my rest and the need for me to drink a lot of water. Mom played Florence Nightingale all over again.

Even though I started feeling stronger, my stomach now acted as if it was strapped to a roller coaster. I kept throwing up what few morsels I had managed to swallow. But not in the house. Dad had installed a doggie door for the shelties, and I learned to use it my first day at home. Now, I needed it. A lot. Whenever I had the urge, I would struggle outside and head for the soft dirt behind the swimming pool. I'd dig a shallow hole and then vomit into it. As soon as I caught my breath, I'd kick dirt over the stinky mess and return to the house.

Mom or Dad always followed me when I wobbled out. After the second or third episode, I overheard them discussing how I covered my throw-up remains. Dad chuckled "He's not half house cat is he?"

When Mom's friends called and asked about my progress, they were amazed when she mentioned my burying routine. Dad described it when we visited the vet, but the doc said he never heard of such a thing. I don't think the guy believed him.

Hey, digging a hole was the couth thing to do. First of all, no way I'd dirty the house. And I didn't want to be responsible for the other dogs getting sick, not even Diamond.

Even though I slept a lot, I had time to think. And when I awoke one morning, it hit me about what Dad had said a few days earlier. "He's not going anywhere." There was no mistake in what he meant. They were going to adopt me. It was the best medicine I could have been given. The people I've been labeling as Foster Mom and Foster Dad, would be my *real* Mom and Dad.

My crisis had turned out to be a blessing. And thankfully Mother Nature didn't give me tear ducts because I would have flooded the house with tears of joy.

The vet said I had turned the corner and was on the path to recovery. And only I knew the remedy that did it. Love!

But when Mom and Dad began feeding me human baby food as the vet had suggested, I couldn't keep it down and lost all my desire to eat. Back to the veterinarian I went. My withered body now looked like I'd spent weeks stranded on a life raft in the Indian Ocean. On the way out of the veterinarian's office I heard him tell Mom, "I think we're going to run out of dog."

Peggy, a dear friend of Mom's, came by to see me and she mentioned that one of her dogs couldn't digest chicken. Her vet said it was a common food allergy with dogs.

"Chicken?" Mom shouted, "That's what we've been feeding the baby." She yelled for Dad and told him what Peggy had said. Tires squealed as the car peeled out of the driveway and in a few minutes, Dad returned with jars of Gerber's beef baby food.

I gobbled a tablespoon every half-hour. Mom gradually

increased the portions and after several days, I devoured several jars of beef at a time. Bottom line? I also had a chicken allergy. Within a few weeks my normal energy had returned, and I was growing closer to Geoff's size, maybe fifty pounds.

When Mom and Dad formally adopted me, the people at the Humane Society smiled as if they expected it. They were disappointed that my fostering experiment had ended but were happy that I had a good home. Knowing that I had become a member of a human family greatly reduced my anxiety about being returned to the shelter. Yet I had learned that nothing was certain in life. Would they tire of me? Or would my medical expenses be a financial burden and they couldn't afford to keep me? Trade me in for a more cuddly puppy? I knew one thing for sure. I wasn't going to do anything destructive around the house.

But my stomach flipped a few times when I first thought about Diamond being a sibling. However I had grown larger than her so when she aimed her barking complaints at me I was no longer intimidated.

While Dad continued to talk up the foster training idea at board meetings, the experiment had ended at our house. My human parents now had four permanent canines roaming the halls, and they agreed that was enough.

"God sat down for a moment when the dog was finished in order to watch it, and to know that it was good, that nothing was lacking, that it could not have been made better."

Rainer Maria Rilke

CHAPTER

7

A HERO'S DREAM

I was growing fast, and Mom started describing me as a guy wearing snowshoes. In spite of my large paws though, I was cute. I dressed in a golden strawberry coat, a noble black muzzle, and long soft ears.

Ever since Mom pointed out the narrow ridge of hair along my spine, and my size and temperament, she considered me a Rhodesian Ridgeback. And I knew the Ridgeback stock came from Africa, were brave, and bred to hunt lions. Sounded pretty cool.

But I brushed off the lion hunting talk because no way would I go to Africa and hunt one of those guys. Then one afternoon Mom and I watched a National Geographic program about lions competing for food in the county's southern grasslands. Man, it's a tough place to live. That evening I thought about the TV program. I kept wondering how I would react if a lion jumped me? Five times my size, a mouthful of ice picks and a roar that sounds like thunder.

I had trouble sleeping that night. When my eyelids finally closed, I found myself hiking on a narrow path near the Zambezi River in Zimbabwe with Dad. The mist from Victoria Falls glistened on the horizon. Barefooted and shirtless, Dad wore an old

Cleveland Indian's baseball cap and a pair of plaid cargo shorts. He toted a walking stick about the size of a broom handle. A broom handle is adequate to defend yourself from an attacking chipmunk or even a squirrel. But in Africa? Most of the creatures lurking around there would use it as a toothpick. And you know who they would be picking out of their teeth.

Sometimes the river would be in view and then disappear as it wove through a mass of multicolored grasses in the marshland. A gentle breeze swayed the leafy vegetation, like some breathing monster waiting to pounce on unsuspecting prey. As we followed the path over a small hill we saw a magnificent wide stretch of the Zambezi's blue-green water rippling toward the Indian Ocean, its ultimate destination.

The grasses tapered to ankle height, and then a small sandy beach along the river appeared. A hippo family played in a deep pool. Watching the huge bodies dive and splash in the water conjured my own call of the wild. But my exhilaration vanished when I spotted a huge crocodile dart into the water.

My mouth felt like someone jammed it full of Texas toast. If I were human, my forehead would have been drenched with nervous sweat. Dad noticed that I was on high alert and leaned to pet me.

"Don't worry, I'll protect you."

Yeah. Now I feel much better.

Then I saw that we weren't the first to visit that spot because someone had left a rope coiled on a rock at the water's edge. The jungle's unusual smells and sights had me on edge, and since I enjoyed playing tug-of-war with Dad, a game now could relieve some of my tension. I dashed toward the rope. It moved. I braked.

26

"Snake!" Dad screamed.

The grayish brown serpent unraveled and slithered toward the water, the tip of its tail ten feet behind the head. Dad grabbed my collar…

Gasping for air, I woke up and wrestled the blanket from around my neck. The bedroom walls appeared to be shaking, but it was me quivering. I sat upright and checked on Mom and Dad. They were sleeping. I closed my eyes. Had to finish my safari.

Dad and I continued along a trail through high grass while squawks and shrieks from unseen birds and animals kept us alert. Ultimately the rumble of Victoria Falls overpowered the jungle voices.

Then the wind shifted, and I caught the whiff of a strange animal. A scent I didn't recognize. My hackles shot up. Then unnatural movement in the undergrowth. Dad froze. A huge head wrapped with a ginger-colored scraggy mane jutted from the grass. The lion's dark eyes glowered, injecting fear toward its prey. Us. Stepping onto the trail, his tail swished back and forth like a whip prepared to crack.

Dad shuffled backward. He whispered something that I didn't understand. Then, his terrified plea. "Chase! Chase, come!"

But I crept forward. A growl rose from deep within me. My Dad wasn't going to become the blue-plate special for some jungle predator. I crouched and let loose a defying, vicious growl. The lion bolted toward me. Our bodies crashed like freight trains colliding. I awoke and staggered to my feet. My dream. How I reacted. A huge underdog, yet I challenged the king. A surge of pride hit me. My subconscious had revealed the real me.

"The greatest fear that dogs know is the fear that you will not come back when you go out the door without them."

Stanley Coren

CHAPTER

8

NOT FOR ME

Despite my frigid relationships with Diamond and Dancer, I must admit they were winners. I had watched the girls compete in the obedience ring a few times and they always did well. As a team, Mom and Dancer won piles of ribbons. Dad and Diamond won a few too. Me? I had become the family's black sheep of the obedience ring.

With Diamond and Dancer, I trained once a week with dozens of humans and their canine companions at the Phoenix Field and Obedience Club. The organized mob met at a park or school ground and practiced their routines. Don't worry, pooper-scoopers were all over the place. Mom was an instructor and of course one of the best. She was also the obedience club's president.

In the ring with Mom, Dancer pranced as if she enjoyed every second of the routine. However, Diamond was the more flamboyant performer. Smart, beautiful and she knew all the commands to perfection. But as a spectator, "Miss Contrarian" spent most of her time barking her complaints to other dogs. The weather was too hot or too cold. The grass too dry or too wet. The judge too tall or too short. Her peers ignored her.

One Saturday morning I sat with Mom at a park to watch Dad and Diamond participate in an obedience competition. I don't know who was more nervous, Mom or me, when the two entered the ring.

They were performing as crisp as soldiers on parade. A ribbon-winning feat. Then, Diamond spotted a young lady enter the park with her canine companion. Bolting from the ring, Diamond sprinted toward them. She nearly reached the duo when like a dive bomber peeled off and headed back to the performance ring. When she returned the spectators clapped and laughed, asking, "what happened?" Dozens of other canines were all around the ring that could have distracted her, but the one Diamond darted after was a Border Collie. Same size and coloring as Geoff.

Without a doubt in my mind, Diamond being Diamond, meant to chew out Geoff for being at the park without her permission. When we got home, I nipped her butt for being such a jerk.

PS–The judge disqualified Dad because Diamond left the ring.

***

I think Mom and Dad had figured out that I loved them, and wanted to be at their side, just not prancing in a roped area with them.

Do you know how it works in the obedience ring? You walk beside your handler until the judge orders, "Halt." And then you must sit. Quickly. Shoulders straight. Ok, fair enough. But as soon as I positioned my backside on the grass, the judge would bellow, "Forward." Protocol demands you promptly rise and get moving again. Left turn. About turn. Slow. Right turn. Run. You do all of it until you churn into butter. The whole thing didn't make a bit of sense. I wasn't a yo-yo.

My slow-motion action didn't endear me to the judges. My report cards had comments like, "Moves like Jell-O, quick as a scarecrow, and performs like he has a hangover." As much as I hate to admit it, they were all valid.

Even though I knew all the routines, formal obedience wasn't for me. Hey, my genes longed to hunt lions in the Serengeti. And the humans want me to strut in a confined roped area like a perfumed French poodle.

Anyhow, I became a part of the obedience club's weekly routine, but for the socializing. I met a lot of nice people and some friendly dogs too. But once I spotted a human slap his German Shepherd because the critter didn't respond to a command. One of the trainers observed it too, and she chewed out the handler like a chunk of rawhide. Hey, think about it. How does hitting anyone teach anything? Maybe fear. Never loyalty or friendship.

More than once, Dad mentioned how studies have shown that people who abuse their dogs often end up doing the same thing to their children and spouses. That's why I think canine mistreatment should be reported, not only for the creatures' benefit, but for the human family too.

The Phoenix Field and Obedience Club also offered agility training classes, and Mom taught them too. And I had learned all the agility exercises during Sunshine School's advanced puppy class, and they were more fun than the obedience drills.

Do you know the challenges? Up and then down a teeter-totter, clear a broad jump, then a high jump, climb up and down a six foot high A-frame, and go through a long plastic tunnel. It also included a line of narrow poles we had to weave through. The poles were a problem for a big-bodied guy like me, and Dad said I looked like an eighteen-wheeler trying to park in our garage.

One steamy night after a training class, I heard Mom brag about how well I performed the agility drills at home. So while the equipment was still set up, she gathered her friends and expected me to act like a circus elephant.

To please her, I hustled through the tunnel, up one side of the teeter-totter and down the other. Mom gloated. The next challenge required going up a ramp to a long board, walk across it, and then go down the back ramp.

I plopped at the foot of the front ramp and wouldn't budge. I'd decided this performance stuff wasn't in my genes.

Mom tried to coax me with kind words and then bribe me with chunks of dried liver. I gobbled the liver but wouldn't budge. She touched my nose with a piece of the meat and placed it on the middle of the board. I could feel the magnetic pull. Maybe like a teenage boy struggling to keep his eyes closed to a Playboy centerfold.

But I resisted.

Mom wrinkled her nose and muttered, Stinker." She trotted over to unleash Diamond so she could remind me how to finish the exercise. When Mom returned with Diamond in tow, she saw me sitting at the middle of the board. I threw her a mischievous smile while I enjoyed the petting from three cute, laughing ladies.

"A dog is not 'almost human,' and I know of no greater insult to the canine race than to describe it as such."

John Holmes

CHAPTER

9

GEOFF

As I mentioned before, Mom and Dancer must have been ordained to perform together in the obedience ring. Dancer possessed the loyalty and willingness to please, and Mom was endowed with the patience and expertise to effectively train.

Dancer's cumulative winnings had earned her a Utility Dog title, the top rung of the obedience ladder. With no other obedience mountains to conquer, and since Shelties were originally bred to shepherd sheep, Mom decided to test Dancer's herding genes.

Obedience competition rewards side-by-side, human-canine precision routines in a confined area. Herding requires the duo to split up, while working as a team in large open pastures.

Here's how sheep trials work as I understand them. The course set-up represents the herding tasks that a sheep farmer and his dog need to manage the stock. That includes gathering the sheep, driving, shedding, and penning. Competitive shedding is the act of isolating one marked sheep from the others.

To start, with an empty pen nearby, the handler and dog stand next to a post at one end of the pasture. A judge is positioned nearby. A small flock, generally five or six sheep, is approximately fifty yards out. The handler must direct her dog by using hand, voice, or whistle commands.

The dog is sent to the sheep with commands to steer them back to the handler and around the post. Then they're sent out again and through a pair of gates stationed midway in the pasture. Once the sheep pass through the gates the dog is directed to shed the marked sheep from the others. After the shedding, and the marked sheep is held away from the others for a short time, the dog must then regroup the sheep and direct them into the pen.

A short explanation for scoring is that each competitor starts with 15 minutes and 100 points. Points are ducted if the sheep do not precede through the required positions along the competitive route, and within the time allotment. I think you get the idea. Challenging to say the least.

Through networking in the dog community, Mom met people who volunteered to help get her started on the craft of sheep herding. However, they told Mom that to improve her chances to be a winner she needed the Corvette of sheep dogs, a Border Collie. Not a Volkswagen Beatle like a Sheltie.

Mom did her homework, and she located three or four reputable Border Collie breeders in Arizona. She visited several and decided upon a male puppy whose father had been a champion herding dog. She named the pup Geoff.

So, now you know that Geoff's role was to team up with Mom and help her cover another wall with blue ribbons. But because of Geoff's youth, the experts said to keep him on the sidelines until he had physically and emotionally matured. Mom planned to give Dancer a try at herding and together they would learn the verbal commands and how to read the sheep's body language. By then Geoff should be ready to begin his training.

To train Dancer properly, Mom needed a pasture and, of course, sheep. With the help of friends she found a small patch across town where the owner would allow her to keep sheep. So far, so good. Mom then purchased a handful of the large, black faced wool-bearing sheep that were prominent on sheep farms, and therefore used for herding competitions. Made sense to me.

Understandably, most woollies resisted having a canine steer them across a pasture, around obstacles and into a pen. Therefore, the sheep's often haphazard behavior demanded that the handler quickly analyze their movements then shout or whistle instructions to her teammate. The dog must react to the commands or risk creating a sheep wreck.

Mom invited me to observe Dancer's first training session. I saw that she was struggling. To be fair, she'd probably not even seen sheep before and was so small she could run under their bellies. The critters used their bigger bodies to intimidate her, and all her barking wasn't going to make them move if they weren't willing.

After a few minutes of watching the abuse, I couldn't take it. I bolted toward the biggest ewe, the one who bullied my house mate the most. And I found out that sheep can almost climb fences.

After that I had to watch while wearing my leash and hooked to a fence pole.

After consulting with a herding associate, Mom exchanged the burly critters for a flock of Barbados sheep. They look and act like small deer. Experienced trainers prefer Barbados because they're smaller, more agile and therefore more challenging for the dogs. The theory was if your dog could control the Barbados, handling the larger but slower wooly sheep would be a piece of cake.

Learning the hand signals were simple for Dancer, but the voice and whistle commands were more difficult for her. However reading and reacting to the darting moves of the sheep, in the heat of battle, became the major challenge for both Dancer and Mom. It didn't take long to see that herding sheep was about 179 degrees from obedience competition.

In the end, even the smaller Barbados rebelled, and Dancer would race to Mom's side. Her lack of size and confidence resulted in a haphazard style that headed nowhere. Dancer's herding genes were nonexistent. Not surprising. The Shetland Sheepdog had become known for their obedience successes and for generations had been bred for the ring competition. Despite Dancer's herding failure, the sport hooked Mom and most importantly, she could still work with canines. What else could a human want?

Mom slowly exposed Geoff to her flock, and as he grew into a young adult, she began his training in earnest. When I went with Mom and Geoff to the pasture, I'd listen to Mom shout directions to Geoff: "Come by," and "Away to me." Scottish talk, but in simple English they meant circle right or left.

In an instant I could see that the flock reacted much differently to Geoff. First, he was much bigger and covered ground in a flash. But the most obvious thing was his technique, his eye. He would slink toward them, his eyes watching every movement, burning a hole into their souls, daring them to step out of line. I must admit his style even got my attention.

Question. What's so hard about training someone? I always managed to get Dad to do whatever I wanted.

Then I noticed that depending on which side of the bed Geoff got up, his morning's training session could become a unique adventure. That made the sport an unexpected challenge for Mom. Geoff had his good days but inconsistency had become his middle name. Too often when she gave him a direction he'd just run helter-skelter after the sheep. No one got hurt, but at times he had the woollies jumping in all directions like hail bouncing off

Dad's bald head.

In all fairness to Geoff, I thought the small pasture with little room for maneuvering the sheep was a major part of the problem. Plus, the sheep had figured out the modus operandi. As soon as Mom shouted her first command to Geoff they ran directly into the pen.

Deciding that they needed a larger area to effectively train, Mom and Geoff played Lawrence of Arabia. That is, they traveled like nomads to her herding friends' larger pastures and worked with different flocks.

Along the way Mom found a professional to help improve her training skills. He lived in Cordes Junction, about seventy-five miles from home. I joined them once and I remember one exercise when Mom instructed Geoff to move the sheep behind a knoll and back to her. They disappeared behind the small hill, and after about thirty seconds, the well-organized flock reappeared with Geoff in charge. A great performance. A drill sergeant couldn't have had better command, and I must admit I was proud of him.

But after a few more months, Mom was doubting Geoff's potential. And her own. She discussed her concerns with her trainer and herding friends. They all said be patient.

"To be a top handler it takes about ten years to read and respond the various antics of the sheep," the trainer said. "Experience is the sole teacher. Don't forget, it's also frustrating for the canine to be directed by a neophyte handler."

"Dogs are our link to paradise. They don't know evil or jealousy or discontent. To sit with a dog on a hillside on a glorious afternoon is to be back in Eden, where doing nothing was not boring—it was peace."

Milan Kundera

CHAPTER

10

ANSWER MAN

Mom realized that I understood what it took to be an effective herding dog. So, when she became the editor for the Arizona Herding Association newsletter, she thought that I could help other dogs with their training issues. She introduced a monthly column where I'd play Dear Abby, and answer queries submitted by the canine community.

Looking back, most came from canines who had a variety of questions. I thought you might be interested in reading some of my favorites.

Dear Chase,

I have a breed championship, a few obedience blue ribbons, a tracking title and one in agility too. I want to be well rounded. Do you think I can get a herding ribbon before the spring herding competitions?

Anxiously awaiting your reply,

Chico (I'm a three-year-old Chihuahua)

Dear Chico,

The spring of which century did you have in mind? I know I give the Border Collies a bad time, but they are big, fast, and smart hombres. Learning the intricacies of herding is difficult even for them and few are successful. I'm impressed with your achievements, but you need three things to be a successful herding dog. They are genes, genes, and genes.

I don't want to discourage you, but if you must, my suggestion is to gain about fifty pounds, move to Scotland and hook up with an experienced handler.

Good Luck,

Chase

Off the record, I don't believe much of what Chico said. I don't remember even seeing one Chihuahua train for any type of competition let alone win a ribbon.

Dear Chase,

I know your specialty is sheep herding, but my master has started college and needs some ideas for a research project in his civil engineering class. I know you can help.

Heinz (I'm 3/16 Wolf Hound, 1/8 Dachshund, 3/8 Vizsla and 1/4 Bulldog)

Dear Heinz,

I think he should decide on a subject that has a historic design and yet possesses artistic lines. Professors like the lines. The Pyramid of Khufu in Egypt is one. It was completed in 2600 B. C. (that doesn't mean Border Collie). You can't go wrong with St. Peter's Basilica, but a lot of students pick that one. My favorite study is the Suez Canal, but if you want to go American, try the Brooklyn Bridge.

Best Always,

Chase

PS - Check your math, unless you have a bobbed tail, your genes are 1/16 short.

As you can see by my responses, I tried to be accommodating. Some asked pretty stupid questions, especially the humans. But there were some benefits too.

Dearest Chase,

I saw your picture on the Humane Society Christmas Card. I think you're really handsome. Could you give me your phone number so that maybe we could share a treat sometime?

Very Sincerely,

Fluffy (I'm a two-year-old Puli)

Dear Fluffy,

It's against Arizona Herding Association policy to use this column for personal purposes, but there are exceptions to any policy. My number is 555-12324. Call any time.

Very, Very Sincerely,

Chase

I kept statistics about my column. You know, number of letters every month, how many from canines and from humans, stuff like that. But Fluffy's reply got me in trouble with Dad. By including our phone number in my answer to her, I received 205 calls from different gals. In 48 hours. Dad had to unplug the phone and then change our number.

Afterward I heard Dad laughing when he told a neighbor about it. Said that the ringing sounded like Christmas with *Jingle Bells* being played around the clock. I should explain Fluffy's Christmas card comment. The Humane Society's Board of Directors constantly searched for new sources of income to help pay for animal care. Dad proposed that they print and sell Christmas cards that included the holiday greetings, but also a message about pet overpopulation.

He suggested that the face of the card should represent the Arizona Humane Society and be one of its alumni. And, like magic, while a committee discussed the card format, a perfect model for the project popped (popped or planned) into Dad's head–me.

Mom gave an artist friend, John, several of my pictures and he drew a freehand rendition of me. Handsome result. (John had a lot to work with.) But, to my dismay, he sketched a kitten in my arms. A feline. And to top it off he painted a huge red bow around my neck.

The canines at home teased me for months about my transformation from a lion hunter to a kitty babysitter. Just jealous. Anyhow, many of the irresistible Christmas cards were sold, and that's where Fluffy found my picture.

**"Dogs are not our whole life,
but they make our lives whole."**

Roger Caras

CHAPTER

11

COMING OF AGE

Mom and Dad decided I needed a specific birth date. And since I was born in July, they declared that the fourth would be the big day. They said it fit. Something about freedom from the animal shelter.

Birthdays are supposed to be fun, with everyone eating cake and ice cream. But on that night as it was getting dark, rockets, firecrackers and sparklers lit the sky at our neighborhood park. Dad insisted that the celebration was for me. Yeah, sure. Even as a one-year-old, I knew that the ruckus wouldn't be for a canine birthday.

It must have had another meaning. Maybe to celebrate something important, like all the dogs had escaped from the shelter. I hope that's it.

Anyhow, Dad and I took a walk to the park, and I remember the sidewalk felt like a heating blanket. Normally we took our summer outings in the morning before the sun baked the sidewalk, but Dad wanted me to see the nighttime festivity. As we strolled, the sky lit up every few seconds with beautiful shades of red, brilliant whites and glowing blues. I could see Dad smiling at me from the light of the rockets' red glare.

But along the way we heard frightened dogs whine and howl, upset by the booming, weird noises. And I knew that most of them wouldn't calm down for the rest of the night. I had jumped at the sound of the first blast, but with Dad at my side I regained my composure and enjoyed the colorful displays.

When we returned home, I saw that my canine family endured the ruckus by staying close to Mom. Then I spotted small bowls of vanilla ice cream with embedded doggy treats lining the kitchen countertop. Mom gave us a sit-stay command and placed the refreshments at different locations on the floor. Then she and Dad sang happy birthday to me while the goodies were devoured.

After we exchanged licking each other's empty bowls, Dad led me into the bedroom. Choked by a huge blue bow, a stuffed African lion snuggled in my bed. Mom said the toy was a present from Diamond because she loved me. Sure, but I would've rather had a hamburger. And if I had a penny each time she snapped at me, I could have bought a pride of real lions. Maybe the whole Phoenix Zoo.

But sometimes even a walk can be embarrassing. Shortly after my birthday, Dad clipped my collar to one of the Sheltie leather leashes, and we headed to the park. We were about halfway and I was ogling a beautiful golden retriever walking across the street when the wind shifted. A strong, fresh feline odor hit me. Right between the eyes–my nose. Yeah. Like a hammer from a Tom and Jerry cartoon. The cat had to be lurking in the oleanders bordering the sidewalk. Watching. Calculating my moves. I lunged into an opening. The leash snapped.

A calico cat sat atop a block wall behind the bushes, sneering at me. Then with its tail dangling just out of my reach, it started licking its paw. As if adding another canine to its chump's list.

The next day I had a new leash of my own. More like a horse's rope lead. You know, the kind you snap onto a bridle of a 500-pound critter. Dad said I was as big as a colt, so he'd treat me like one.

***

Mom tended to Geoff and the Shelties, so that left Dad and me to do things together. We were a team when we did the obedience stuff, but he took it more seriously than I did. Besides, you'll never hear me agree that being on a leash and taking orders was fun. So, our obedience team kind of disbanded after I kept chewing up the leashes.

The pool activities were relaxing but after a while they became boring, and I wanted something more macho. My puppy maladies were ancient history and by now, I had grown into a marvelous specimen of canine manhood. I'm not boasting. A fact is a fact. I was from the stock of a rugged breed, weighed about ninety pounds and was full of energy.

Hey, don't all teenage guys physically test their dads now and then? So, outside one day when we were on the back lawn, I swung a paw toward my Old Man, like a Muhammad Ali jab. And he got the message. Dad had wrestled in college and after thirty years or so he still weighed the same. He wanted to see if he still had the moves. I wanted to show that I had some alpha in me. So we went at it.

Rules? Only one. No blood. But I think even the Marquess of Queensberry couldn't have watched one of our tussles without wincing a few dozen times.

We faced off with Dad on his knees and his hands on the ground. I danced a few steps, then bowled into him and tried to knock him on his butt. He turned to one side and managed to twist behind me. He had the advantage of hands and he put a half Nelson on me while I squirmed and flailed. But when I got the opportunity, I used my best weapon—my mouth. I'd grip his wrist, a perfect fit, and it had that yummy, bony feeling.

The longer we wrestled the rougher it got. Dad never gouged my eyes like they do on TV. But I'm not saying you could call him an angel. I'd get my tail pulled, then my ears. And in between he tickled my armpits. (I admit I'm ticklish.) Dad even pulled a Mike Tyson once. Mom witnessed it. She'll testify. He bit my ear.

Yeah, I inadvertently scratched him from time to time, but he was a good sport about it. And scratches quickly heal. On occasion, he got indented. Yeah, indented. Dad had a different word for it though. He called it a bite-mark. But he didn't accuse me of being an alligator since I never broke the skin. But the first time Mom noticed his arms after one of our matches she said, "What an original tattoo. An impression of a dog's mouth on your forearm."

So, what are the differences between indentations and bite marks? It's a matter of semantics. One man's hero was another person's mugger. Anyhow, we both had fun.

"Dogs' lives are too short.
Their only fault, really."

Agnes Sligh Turnbull

CHAPTER

12

THE WINDFALL

When a larger bank acquired the one where Dad worked, life at home suddenly became chaotic. It appeared inevitable that organizational changes would be made and he could be impacted. He had recently celebrated his 55th birthday and became eligible for early retirement.

What if Dad retired? Mom had sold her technical writing business years before and so she had no professional ties to worry about. She had spent her childhood in Maryland and longed to live once again in a cooler, greener countryside.

Could we move to the Garden of Eden Mom had dreamed about? A home with large, lush pastures to train her Border Collies? And mountain forests for me to roam and explore? If we did, Mom suggested that after Dad scrubbed the kennels, cleaned the barn, mended the fences, manicured the yard, and helped care for the sheep, he could squeeze in a round of golf.

Of course, Mom was teasing him.

However, I had serious concerns. I watched the nightly news. Banks were merging or being gobbled up in hostile takeovers.

What if the new owners of Dad's bank cut him loose? No job. No money. No Chase?

I couldn't avoid my negative thoughts about going back to the shelter. Yes, I knew my humans loved me, but who knows? Tough times often result in tough decisions and families split up. I was a rescue dog, picked because of the color of my coat.

For weeks, my human parents acted edgy as the discussions continued at the bank about Dad's future. He would come home from work with a smile one evening and a frown the next. During the day, Mom drifted around the house hoping for the phone to ring and hear Dad say that we won the lottery with a generous buyout.

On a November Friday afternoon the phone rang. Dad's voice bellowed, "We got it. More than we hoped!" The dream had come true. He had been given a substantial severance package. My worries evaporated. Mom bounced around the house like a puppy with a new toy. She asked me to dance. I refused. None of that hip swing stuff for me. I only do the foxtrot.

His retirement would be effective at the end of the year. Now the pursuit of paradise began in earnest. For several years Mom and Dad had been taking their vacations throughout the neighboring states to find the perfect location to live out their years. They said no to New Mexico, generally as hot and dry as Arizona. Colorado? Too cold. California? Too expensive.

The Rogue Valley of Southern Oregon fit all their expectations. It had four relatively pleasant seasons, modest rainfall, and was surrounded by scenic pine and oak covered mountains. Mom said it would be like living in the palm of God's hand.

With the decision made, Mom told friends about our Oregon

plans. The next day the doorbell rang. The word had spread about our move, and a neighbor's family member was interested in buying our house. Mom and Dad sold it two days later.

So in April, with all of the family canines safely housed with friends, Mom and Dad headed to Oregon to find us a new home. It seemed like forever, but two weeks later, they returned with pictures of the small farm they bought outside of Medford, Oregon. They spread the photos on the floor so I could see my new home. The place looked beautiful. And heading toward the prime of my life, ready for a new adventure, I couldn't wait to get there.

Mom's parents had died years ago as did Dad's father. But his mother lived by herself a few miles from our Phoenix home. She was eighty years old and couldn't hear, not even a barking Sheltie. Dad explained our plan to her and that he wanted her to come with us. Thankfully she agreed, and without argument. She had always treated me well, and so I was glad she was coming with us.

***

A wave of sadness swept over me as I thought about leaving Phoenix. Somewhere in the Valley of the Sun lived my birth parents and I often wondered if they ever thought about me. I had hoped to meet them someday. What did my father look like? A purebred Ridgeback? Big chested, strong and brave? My mother a Ridgeback mix? Sweet and lovable?

I had a lot of friends from the Sunshine puppy classes and I'd miss them too.

Mom and Dad said I'd like Oregon and the smell of fresh pine trees with room to run and exciting places to hike. That meant wildlife trails and the opportunity to practice my hound skills. No African lions of course. And I knew Mom and Dad wouldn't let me harm any wild animal.

They said Oregon would be a cooler and more comfortable place to live, and I'd get to play in snow. A place cooler than Phoenix appealed to me, but snow? I watched a National Geographic TV program one time about Alaska and learned all about snow and ice. Not sure I'd like that.

Shetland Shelties with their long coats descended from somewhere below the Arctic Circle and wouldn't worry about the cold. I think Geoff was born in Siberia. He'd always jump into the coldest water he could find to cool off after a workout. But remember, my distant relatives came from Rhodesia (now Zimbabwe), a warm twenty degrees latitude below the equator. And who ever heard of a Zimbabwe Ridgeback? And why change the country's name?

Dad wasn't sure about the name change but he knew someone in our neighborhood who might know. While on a walk one Saturday morning we stopped to meet a gentleman who was from South Africa. He had conducted photography safaris in the region.

I sat at Dad's side as the man explained that Rhodesia had had internal unrest and fighting for years. It withdrew from the Commonwealth of Nations in 1965, and in 1980 it was renamed Zimbabwe. As I sat there and listened to the man talk, it didn't sound like a nice place to live.

So, no name change for me. I'll stick to my Rhodesian Ridgeback title and my USA home.

"If I have any beliefs about immortality,
it is that certain dogs I have known will go to heaven,
and very, very few persons."

James Thurber

CHAPTER

13

A NEW LIFE

By May, we were living on West Griffin Creek Road in Medford, Oregon on a two-acre farm. Laura remained in Arizona to continue her college studies.

The farm was laid out in three sections with wire fencing defining each part. The north side pasture, about an acre in size, spread across the front of the property and ran parallel to the road. In the middle part sat our ranch-style house, a small barn and a grove of oak, pine and madrone trees. Behind the middle section was a second and a smaller pasture.

A combination of wood and wire fencing bordered the whole property.

Curving down from the road to the house was a long driveway with a sturdy gate mounted about midway. It kept all the canines safely confined. Mom's land management plan was to train the sheep on both pastures until the hay growing season, then restrict her training to the rear pasture. Both were gated and off limits to all canines unless accompanied by Mom or Dad.

Dad's idea was to build an apartment for Grandma that would

provide her own space and privacy. Our garage was connected to the east side of the house, and the apartment would be attached to the east side of the garage.

Dad showed the floor plan to Grandma, Mom, and me. The front door faced west and toward the front of the house. The kitchen, with a work and storage island, occupied a corner of the main, open room. The bedroom had a large closet and an oversized bathroom. A bedroom exit opened into our garage and from there she could enter the house. The back door of the garage led to a set of steps and toward the barn.

Grandma's view to the north would be from a cozy bay window. Probably where she would place her table for eating, and a spot to give me leftovers and treats. Her view would take in our front pasture and the neighbor's horses that grazed on the hillside across the road. Out of her eastside windows, she could gaze at a beautifully manicured peach orchard and the green rolling hills beyond the fruit trees.

All in all, a cute, practical setup. And most importantly, Grandma loved it. She would live in the house with us until the carpenters completed her apartment.

My job was chief of household security. Dad never put it in writing, but I got the message and accepted the responsibility. So, I spent my free time under the leafy oak trees to figure out a site security strategy. I got my best ideas when I napped. They were like Native American vision quests, and the dreams often helped me map things out.

The previous owners owned horses, and the big guys had damaged the fences when they gnawed on the wooden posts or scratched their butts on the wire fencing. I decided that my first duty was to find the holes in the fences. Then I'd regularly check the openings to discourage intruders until Dad repaired them.

West Griffin Creek Road led down from the western mountains and provided a scenic pathway to the valley floor in Medford. Because of the rural setting there wasn't a lot of traffic, but some drivers would speed. And on occasion people would ride their bicycles past our house.

I had decided that my first line of defense should not be our front door, but at the driveway gate. Generally, strangers were persona non grata (I learned that term on the Court Channel). So, whenever someone cycled or even walked along West Griffin Creek, I hustled to the gate. In a firm but polite bark, I'd let them know that they needed my okay before they could approach our house.

By the way, I'm not a creature who's glued to the TV. But because of Phoenix's summer heat, I stayed in the house a lot and usually watched television. No soap operas though. I insisted on the more educational channels.

Mom and Dad would know if we had gate-side visitors because the volume of my bark would raise a few hundred decibels. My policy was, "by appointment only." No exceptions. So if I didn't recognize them I'd slap my paws on top of the gate, elevate my hackles, display pearly white teeth and spray them with spittle.

I had accepted my security job on a 24/7 basis, and that's how I earned my keep. Geoff was there to learn sheep herding and the shelties were supposed to, well, I don't know what their role was. Mom reminded me that they were sheep herding dogs too, just over the hill. I don't know which hill she meant, but how about the farthest hill?

I did have one incident though, and not so much about security, but I'll give an example of how I react when challenged. It happened when workmen were constructing Grandma's apartment and Dad drove into town to get some stuff at the hardware store. That meant I was the man of the house and in charge.

The carpenters worked on the framing, doing their pounding, sawing, and swearing when the ugly black and orange van pulled up. The plumbers. Two of them. One talked to me and patted my head. Okay. Nice guy. Plumber number two scooted by and shot a dirty look my way. He did the same thing a second time. Like warning me not to use his boot as a fire hydrant, as if I'd do anything that uncouth. Then, he hustled by with a long piece of pipe. Not PVC, but real iron pipe. He swung it like he was swatting mosquitoes and missed my head by a hair. An unprovoked warning shot across my brow.

What choice did I have? If someone takes a swing at the site security guard, it's a matter of duty, self-defense, and self-respect. So, I nipped his butt. No blood. No skin tear. Just wanted to give the bozo a heads up. The worst part, his jeans tasted like rotten catfish.

Alan, the boss guy on the job and my buddy, heard the man yelp. He stepped in and calmed the guy. I guess the plumber could have caused a lot of trouble for Mom and Dad, and especially me, but nothing ever came of it. I overheard Alan tell Mom about it, but I don't know if she told Dad. At least he never said anything to me about the incident. But if he knew the facts, he'd back me 100 percent.

Keep in mind that I had a perfect record while I was Chief of Security. Not one bad guy got onto the property while we lived there. I didn't receive any medals. No Purple Heart or even one of those red and white Good Conduct ones, but I know our family appreciated my service.

"The animals of the planet are in desperate peril, without free animal life I believe we will lose the spiritual equivalent of oxygen."

Alice Walker

CHAPTER

14

MY ACHING BACK

Soon after we arrived in Oregon, Mom and Dad sought a reputable veterinarian to care for our canine family. They were especially concerned about me because my gait had become abnormal. One of our new neighbors, Jean, had several dogs and she recommended a vet named Dale, and Mom made an appointment with him.

After meeting and discussing my medical history with Dr. Dale, he wanted to see me run. So Dad and I jogged a lap around the parking lot while the vet watched me. I tried to stride naturally but both hips shouted slower, slower until thankfully the run ended.

As we headed back to his office, I heard him tell Dad, "Chase's trotting method makes it clear that he has problems with both hips. He should have been taking longer more graceful strides instead of the short, choppy steps that we observed. We need X-rays so we can clearly identify the big guy's problem."

What a nightmare that turned out to be. They lifted me onto a large examination table and tried to get me into the proper position for the X-rays. I didn't growl or bite, but I thought about nipping an assistant's arm as a warning to be careful. My squirming, along with their pushing and pulling made the procedure painful. They made a pretzel out of my right leg. Then the same to my left. Dad kept talking to me as he patted my head, but I couldn't wait to get my four on the floor.

Mom, Dad and I went out to the waiting room, and in a few minutes we were called back into the vet's office. "The X-rays show cartilage degeneration in both hips," said Dr. Dale. "And at some point soon, Chase will have bone rubbing on bone."

I got it. Eventually I would have more pain than I have now.

Dr. Dale rubbed my neck. "The root problem is hip dysplasia. The X-rays reveal it to be more severe than I would have guessed by watching Chase jog."

Dad smiled. "He's a brave guy and doesn't complain. But what about hip replacements?"

Whoa. I needed to hear more about that. Would I be running around with a pair of dachshund's legs? With a configuration like that, I'd look like I was on a permanent sit, even when I'd run. I'd rather swim to Africa and take my chances of surviving on the Serengeti.

I appreciated that Dad recognized I tried not to act like a baby and complain. Yet, an old concern of mine about the cost of my medical problems resurfaced again. Human medical expenses drove some people into bankruptcy, and my medical file already weighed as much as a case of dog food. The family loved me, no doubt about that. But how long would they continue to pay for my bills?

"Historically," said Dr. Dale, "hip replacement success rates with dogs Chase's size aren't good. It's too hard to keep them immobilized." He leaned to massage my ear. "Plus, their body weight puts too much stress on the replacement area and it rarely heals properly. I wouldn't recommend the procedure for him."

I was glad to hear that. No cutting or sawing on me. But what's the alternative? Not the needle! I know that's what happens when vets run out of options. Euthanasia. I've heard what people sometimes talk about in the waiting rooms.

"We've been giving him an over-the-counter glucosamine supplement to help rebuild his joint tissues," said Mom.

"Good, I suggest you continue it," said Dr. Dale, "and we'll add Rimadyl, an anti-inflammatory drug. It will make Chase more comfortable. But there's a risk of long-term side effects with some of these medications, so we'll have to keep a close eye on his progress."

Mom and Dad agreed with the doc's recommendation. And so did I. I'll take a pill over surgery anytime. Are they meat flavored?

**"It's not the size of the dog in the fight,
it's the size of the fight in the dog."**

Unknown Author

CHAPTER

15

MY NEW TAXI

Mom drove a red, Toyota king cab pickup truck. To make it easier for the dogs to see out its back windows, Dad made a wooden platform and placed it over the seats. Mom would lean the front seat forward and the other dogs would jump onto the platform and be ready to be chauffeured around town. However, the increased height made it more difficult for me to get in and out. No problem for the others and normally not for me either, but now the effort hurt my hips.

The only other option would be that I'd have to learn to drive her truck. However, my legs were too short and no way could I handle her stick shift. So, when I went anywhere it was with Dad in his car.

He drove a two-year-old, dark red Honda Accord sedan. He'd put an old sheet over the rear seat and took me wherever we needed to go. But even though I could step into the Accord more easily than the pickup, I couldn't get comfortable on the seat. It was just too soft and mushy, like a marshmallow. (I like food metaphors.) If sitting I'd start wobbling when Dad made a turn and if someone saw me they'd think we were having an earthquake. Sometimes I'd stretch flat across the seat but then I couldn't see anything. So why go sightseeing when there's no sight to see?

On a trip to town one day, Dad must have heard me paw the seat as I fussed to make myself comfortable. He watched me in the mirror and saw how I made like the Tower of Pisa. He understood the problem.

Maybe it shouldn't even be mentioned because Dad's solution to my problem was a little over the top. Maybe way over. Some humans, if they knew the truth, would call Dad crazy.

After we returned home, he told Mom we needed a new car.

"The Honda doesn't even have twenty-seven thousand miles," she said. Her response sounded like a shout. I watched Dad work on her the next few days. He said stuff like, "Got to think ahead. The winter months. Driving in the snow and rain will be a lot more difficult than on the Phoenix sunbaked streets. We need an all-wheel-drive vehicle of some kind. Safer for us, safer for our passengers."

In a few days Mom swung from an adamant "no," to a "I'll think about it." Soon, she slipped into a pleasant sounding "maybe" and finally gave the okay.

The next week we had a new, red all-wheel drive Subaru station wagon. A hatchback with an easy step up for me to get in. With the back seat down, I had a spacious area with a firm base so I could comfortably sit, see the sights and watch the crazy drivers.

A few days later I went some place with Mom and Dad. I don't remember where we were headed but rain drops suddenly splattered our windshield. Dad flipped on the wipers, turned to me, winked, and said to Mom, "Don't you feel a lot safer with an all-wheel drive?"

"Children and dogs are as necessary to the welfare of the country as Wall Street and the railroads."

Harry S. Truman

CHAPTER

16

SHEEP AND BORDER COLLIES

Once our household members, including Grandma, were settled in Oregon, Mom acquired a flock of 12 sheep. When training she'd divide the sheep into two teams so the dogs would always have a well-rested group to work with.

Rather than get the small, quick moving deer-like Barbados sheep she had in Phoenix, she decided it would be better to buy the larger, wool-bearing sheep. Their slower movements would make it easier for the Border Collies to perfect their herding skills. Besides the nimble Barbados probably would jump over our existing fencing. And Mom told me that Dad would burn down the barn before he would do the back-breaking work of putting up new fencing for the two pastures.

But let's make it clear, I'm not suggesting that Dad did all the work around the place. Mom held her own and took good care of the sheep. Not easy stuff. For example, we had a two-sheep holding pen with guillotine doors at the front and back. After driving two ewes into the pen, Mom would grab one by the neck, and as it squirmed she'd inject worming medicine into its mouth. Then give it a shot in the butt to protect against other potential diseases. She had to do the procedures for all the sheep and do it several times a year. Mom also put tags on the sheep's ears while they were penned and that looked tougher than the worming. Tagging the sheep enabled her to keep track of their ages as well as their medical and lambing histories.

However, Mom and Dad left the shearing of the sheep to an experienced neighborhood man. I couldn't believe how quickly he shaved the flock. It was a work of art. Zip, Zip, and ready for the next one. Dad said it reminded him of getting his first haircut as an army recruit.

Mom had hoped the new setting in Oregon would do wonders for Geoff's herding technique, but it never happened. He displayed a lot of energy when working the sheep, but for me, he earned the nickname of Mr. Inconsistency.

At times he performed flawlessly. On command, he'd dart from Mom's side, gather the flock, and deliver them with the control of a mother duck. Next day, he'd flip his switch and chase the ewes like a sailor pursuing women after being at sea for a year. Maybe Geoff was super-smart, and he didn't want to give the alpha position to a human. Or maybe he didn't have the right temperament for sheep herding.

I didn't like what I was thinking, but I no longer saw my buddy capable of being a successful herding dog.

One sunny morning while Mom worked the sheep with Geoff in the front pasture, I sat at the gate casually observing. Two teenage boys who were walking along the road stopped to watch. Geoff broke from his routine and jogged toward the boys to say hello. The boys laughed, and one hollered, "He's a loser lady. A big loser." As they continued their walk, the boys threw stones at him.

Mom shouted at them. Words I didn't understand. But I darted up to the driveway gate and cut loose with my most vicious barks. Startled, the two guys started running down the road. After a minute of spitting fire at them, I turned and watched Mom leave the pasture and head for the house. She was wiping tears from her eyes.

Months later Mom and Dad traveled to Scotland to watch the annual British Isles' Grand Herding Championship. There they saw the best of the best from Ireland, Scotland, England, and Wales compete for the title. When they returned they told me that they were in awe of some of the dogs' performances, but time after time former blue-ribbon winners couldn't properly complete the course.

I thought about Geoff. Maybe I shouldn't be so negative about his performances. It's a tough sport, and few make it to the top of the ladder. I mean how many baseball-loving kids ever become major league all-stars?

While in Scotland, Mom talked to some grizzled old herders and asked them a lot of questions. Almost all said that ideally she should have three Border Collies in different stages of learning. The younger, less experienced dogs would learn by observing the more experienced.

So Mom hired a handyman to construct housing for Border Collies under the trees behind our house. He assembled three, 4-ft by 8-ft chain-link kennels with brick flooring and topped them with a metal roof. Then he put up a four-foot high field fence around the area for the BCs to run when not in their kennels.

The trees of course helped provide shade and additional shelter for the kennels. Adding protection from the wind and rain, Dad painted, then bolted plywood sheets to the outside walls of the chain-link. Mom bought insulated igloo-shaped dog houses and furnished them with rug flooring. She added beach towels for pillows. Of course I had to visit one. The opening was a little too snug for me to easily get in and out. However, inside it was roomy and cozy.

So, acting on the advice she was given in Scotland, and with help from the local sheep herding grapevine, Mom began the search for another dog. As a result she brought home Jake. He was about a year old, black with blotches of white on his back.

He had been training for a few months with a sheepherder in northern California. I thought he had the skills to be a successful herding dog because he was smart. But was also independent and stubborn. It would be up to Mom to make him a team member.

About that time a herding friend was moving to California and asked Mom if she wanted to buy one of her more reliable Border Collies. She did. Cap, a two-year-old male joined Mom's team as the lead dog of her three herders.

Day one I saw that Cap knew how to herd sheep. After working with him for several weeks, Mom entered him in a trial sponsored by an Australian Shepherd club. The course obstacles were set up in a large corral typical of their breed's normal working area for cattle.

Mom and Cap won! When she told Dad of the victory, he gave her a big hug. And I heard her say, "It's so satisfying to have a dog respond to your directions."

Of course the whole family celebrated with all doggies getting a barbequed hamburger.

With Cap's success, Mom felt more confident and comfortable about her training skills.

With Geoff still living in the house, Mom now had her team and a workable routine. Jake and Cap would spend the night in their igloos, get fed in the morning and then have the run of the fenced kennel yard until their turn to work the sheep with Mom. Depending on Mom's training schedule and other chores, the three Border Collies would roam the area surrounding the house with Dancer, Diamond, and me. But I never saw them relaxing in the sun. They couldn't sit still long enough to appreciate the rays. And that included Geoff.

The BCs enjoyed playing together, especially when the irrigation water was flowing. They'd jump into the ditch, get muddy and generally make a mess of themselves. Since there was an igloo vacancy, Mom decided Geoff should be housed outside with Cap and Jake. The move was made and he appeared more comfortable than ever.

At the rear of the house Mom and Dad had added a two-tier deck that stood about five feet or so above ground level. And it provided me an unobstructed view of the kennels. When I'd go up there to sunbathe, I always made sure the Border Collies could see me. Hey, I wanted to show them how the other half lived. Besides, I had house rights, and since we were all huggable I didn't think it made me part of a caste system like in India. But it didn't hurt to make sure they knew who was top dog.

As it turned out Cap performed like a blue ribbon winner in the enclosed arenas but had difficulty in the wide-open pastures where the sheep had no boundaries. Mom saw that she still had a lot of work to do before they could become a successful sheep herding team. But after a frustrating few months, she painfully returned Cap to his previous owner.

Mom continued to look for a compatible teammate that possessed the skill and temperament that she wanted. And there was no way I could help her with the search.

"Don't accept your dog's admiration as conclusive evidence that you are wonderful."

Ann Landers

CHAPTER

17

HOME SWEET HOME

What were the benefits for living in the house? Well first of all, getting food samples from Mom while she cooked. If Dad complained I was eating too much, Mom would say that I served as her master taster and ensured that the food was edible. Of course she was right. I didn't want Dad eating something that needed an extra pinch of salt or pepper. Besides, I watched the History Channel one morning and learned about ancient emperors and kings who had food tasters. But I guess those guys had other reasons for a taster.

Our kitchen was functional but on the small side and I designated myself to be in charge of cleaning up food spills. Therefore, I inspected the floor while Mom cooked. But weaving around her legs must have been a nuisance because she constantly told me to scat. Once in a blue moon she'd banish me from the kitchen but I'd just conjure up my "poor me" look, she'd sigh, "Oh Chase," and all was forgiven.

At dinner my height enabled me to strategically position myself at the table. As the humans ate, I'd check to see who had the most food remaining on their plate. And timing was crucial. You know that saying? "Out of sight, out of mind." Well, no out of sight for me because I stood out like the Eiffel Tower. But not obnoxious. I mean, who wants a chin resting next to their plate while they're eating? That could have had negative consequences like being thrown out of the house. And I wasn't about to live in an igloo no matter how comfortable it felt.

As Mom and Dad neared the end of their meals, I'd circle the table as if stalking prey. Watching. Waiting. Some would call it intimidation, but I prefer to call it persistence. My technique resulted in getting their last morsel at a 99.2324 percent success rate.

Bedding arrangements were another benefit. I had a large cotton pad to sleep on and a blanket to snuggle into if I got cold. Yet one should always be on the lookout for better things in life. Right?

Our west side porch was adjacent to the master bedroom. It overlooked the neighbor's lush pasture and had a background of mature pine and oak trees. Mom and Dad decided to enclose the porch with large windows and make it into a study for Dad. Then they installed French doors between it and the bedroom.

Dad moved his PC workstation and a few pieces of furniture into the study. While he pecked on his computer keyboard I dozed on the floor. However, I couldn't help but notice how his club chair remained empty. Having unused comfort space made no sense, so one day I altered my routine and climbed onto the chair. I fell asleep and awoke only after Dad walked by and patted me on the head.

Sitting in the chair I'd sometimes gaze through the windows and watch deer graze in pasture, their ears perked and tails fluttering. After a while, with incomparable grace, they would leap over the pasture's fence and disappear into the mountainside trees. A scene I'm sure that Norman Rockwell would have loved to paint.

One afternoon, I heard Dad say to Mom, "I'm not using the chair in the study and since Chase likes it, why not convert it into a bed for him?" She rolled her eyes and said, "It's your hangout and your chair." So, with an old sheet draped over it, I became the proud resident of a feather-cushioned armchair.

So at night I stepped onto my new bed, made a few wiggles and curled up. Very cozy and very warm.

> **"The gift which I am sending you is called a dog,**
> **and is in fact the most precious and**
> **valuable possession of mankind."**
>
> Theodorus Gaza

CHAPTER

18

THE EXPLORER

I realized how much I loved Oregon, and there were times when the mountains with their tall pines and majestic oaks reminded me of my Africa motherland. I learned a lot about Zimbabwe when I watched a story about it on the National Geographic Channel. When they repeated the program, I made a point to watch it again. Both times I got teary-eyed.

Dad enjoyed hiking and he always took me with him. He'd take it slow and easy and I'm sure his casual pace was because of my hips. We'd go out every other day or so and explore abandoned logging roads or remote mountain trails. The hills clogged with trees were much prettier than the red tiled rooftops that blanketed Phoenix.

I relished walking under the baby blue Southern Oregon sky patched with puffy snow white clouds. They'd drift in from the coast, and as they headed east would change shapes like stage actors into fresh costumes. I watched for animal-like clouds, especially African critters.

When a cloud took the form of a lion, I'd conjure a scene where I'd race with my Ridgeback team in pursuit of the jungle king.

Needless to say, I led the chase. The lion's fluffy mane would flow across his muscular shoulders as he ran across the sky. Then, the wind would shift, and my prey would change into a stick of cotton candy.

The old roads were overgrown with weeds but easy on the paws. And there were all kinds of animal smells. I'd practice my hound skills and track a scent to its end, usually to a burrow or the base of a tree. Rarely did we meet other humans, but on occasion we'd spot wild critters. Deer and squirrels were the common sightings, but we never had a violent confrontation with any animal.

The one caution Dad repeated during our hikes was for me to stay away from the poison oak. The bush wasn't a problem for me because I wasn't allergic to the oily leaves. However, the plant's slick film would varnish my coat and when Dad gave me a hug, he would get a rash. One time he got it on his arms so bad they looked like hamburger kebabs ready for the barbeque. After a while I learned to spot the stuff and stayed clear of it even if a rabbit dashed into one.

Dad would let me roam but always kept an eye on me. He always worried that I might get into trouble. The truth of the matter, I watched over him. I don't think he understood how quiet and quick a mountain lion could be. I wasn't a match for one, but I wouldn't stand by and let Dad be its lunch.

So if I got too far away, I'd close the gap and be only seconds away from him if a threat appeared. I was sure Dad would head toward me and as a team maybe we'd scare off a hostile animal. Maybe. You know, like Batman and Robin. I would be Batman of course. Thankfully, we never had to test our roles.

When we got home Dad normally massaged my ears and ran his fingers across my body. Almost acting like a policeman frisking a criminal. I didn't realize until I overheard him tell Mom that he was checking my coat for foxtails and ticks. He was concerned that I might have picked up hitchhikers while we walked. Regardless, you can't have a more pleasant way to end a jaunt than with a massage.

We'd go hiking in the winter months too. Once the snows came, the face of nature changed as if we were transported to another planet. The pine tree needles snatched snow as it fell and formed clumps that from a distance looked like shimmering Christmas tree ornaments. Wind gusts would sprinkle the white powder from the trees like Grandma coating sugar cookies. When knee-deep, the snow felt like walking through waves of milk.

I must admit that I enjoyed trekking across the beautiful snow-coated trees and hills a lot more than I thought I would.

But one time during a summer outing Dad became spooked. We were hiking on an old logging road, and I lagged a short distance behind him. He walked around a curve and froze. Turning, he gave me a hand signal. Down. I did. After a few seconds he slowly backed away, still looking up the road. When he reached me, I sensed his anxiety. He whispered, "Go," and we started jogging toward the car. He kept looking back until we reached the Subaru.

"Two men," Dad told me. "Standing next to a tent. Both had rifles but didn't look like hunters. There for another reason."

At home, he told Mom about the incident. "At a glance I could see that those characters were living there with all the junk around their shelter. Probably growing marijuana nearby. The type of guys when seeing a large animal heading toward them, would shoot without hesitation."

Mom frowned, knelt, and smothered me in a hug. I realized why Dad had been so tense. It was because of me.

"Recollect that the Almighty, who gave the dog to be companion of our pleasures and our toil, hath invested him with a nature noble and incapable of deceit."

Sir Walter Scott

CHAPTER

19

GRANDMA

I had the perfect arrangement with my human family. A nice warm bed and hearty meals. Extra treats from Dad when Mom wasn't around. Goodies from Mom when Dad wasn't looking.

However, once the humans established an eating routine for me, breakfast at eight and dinner at six, I figured that my mealtimes were carved in stone. I always knew when it was time for a meal because my stomach had a natural clock. Dad claimed I had swallowed a Mickey Mouse wristwatch during my puppyhood. Whatever. But humans are not always reliable, especially when it comes to feeding their best friends. Mom and Dad were consistent with most things, but they didn't always feed on time. At least by my standards.

When you have a reservation at a fancy restaurant for seven o'clock, don't show up at eight. Right? I didn't expect beef Wellington every day, but how could they forget serving me? And just out of a can and bag, no less. How complicated is that?

When in a good mood, which was most of the time, I'd allow a five-minute grace period before demanding service. That's reasonable. I mean things happen. Tornados, floods, and earthquakes over eight on the Richter might be an excuse for tardiness. But those acts of nature don't happen in our part of the state. So, if the food did not appear in my bowl after the five minutes, I'd thump on Mom or Dad, whoever stood the closest. I mean if you were being starved to death, wouldn't you do the same thing?

What's a thump? It's a technique I first used on Dad when I was a pup. I don't remember how it started, maybe I learned it from one of the guys at Sunshine School.

I'd let him enjoy his goody until a couple of bites were left then saunter up and stare at him. Sometimes he'd pretend he didn't see me, like humans do at food-sharing time. As if you couldn't see an armadillo swimming in your bowl of chicken soup. So, I'd execute my wrinkled-forehead, deprived expression (Place an accordion beside me and you wouldn't know which was the instrument) and hit Dad's thigh with a paw. Then I would flick my tongue a few times. If he turned his back on me then his butt got the blow. The thump got his attention, and my mouth action told him what I needed. It worked most of the time. No chocolate or candy. House rules. But the final bite of a ham sandwich? A slam dunk.

But anytime Dad would snack, I would move in. I mean we did everything else together, so why not snacking?

Sorry, I got a little sidetracked, because I wanted to tell you about my Grandma. She is a wonderful part of my loving family. And she treated me like her grandson. I mean a real human. I know I was her favorite among all the dogs. You could probably toss Dad into the mix, and I'd still be her pick of the litter. So I'd visit her apartment as often as I could.

Being Italian, Grandma loved to cook and feed anything that walked through her door. Being me, I loved to eat. So, as you could

76

guess, we had a relationship made in heaven. If I was sunbathing on the lawn and the aroma of baked meatloaf, seasoned with garlic salt, came my way, I didn't need my internal clock. I moved out. Double time.

Movies and TV programs often portray Italian grandmas as stout and busty, with their hair fixed in a bun. But not my grandma. I bet I outweighed her. Her hair fell to her shoulders, silver as a nickel. And thankfully, her bun was the real thing. That is, homemade Italian bread. Talk about silver? I struck gold. A grandma who made bread twice a week. When she got out the flour and the rolling pin, I knew yummy times were ahead.

After baking hundreds, maybe thousands of loaves during her lifetime she still couldn't figure out her recipe. "Oh my," she'd say. "I made too much dough." So, what did she do with the leftover? Make doggie-sized cookies and top them with a slice of salami. That's my grandma!

Of course, no thumping for food needed at her apartment. Glance at a banana and like a snake shedding its skin, it was peeled and halfway to my mouth. Only the sun rising in the east was more unfailing than Grandma's response to my starved look.

She prepared a meal for the family at her apartment on Tuesdays–her highlight of the week. I always showed up early in case she needed help with preparing the meal or to clean up if food fell on the floor. All afternoon delicious aromas floated around her apartment and just being there buoyed my morale.

When everyone was seated around the table, she began her mantra. "Eat. Eat." Grandma's words sounded more like a command from a chain-gang boss than polite encouragement. Then she'd repeat it in Italian as if to emphasize her point. *"Mangiare, mangiare."*

When I made solo visits, she told me the same thing. At first though, I thought the words meant that I had mange, you know, the mites that make your hair fall out. It upset me. I mean I knew I didn't have a dermatology problem. Then I got it. She was ordering me to eat. Talked me into it every time. You don't offend grandmas. Right?

When Dad returned from food shopping for Grandma, I'd escort him step-by-step as he lugged the groceries into her apartment. I didn't want any eatable item left in the Subaru or get lost along the way.

She would rummage through the sacks of food to insure he bought everything. That was her claim, but I knew she was searching for my treats that always topped her shopping list. And they were the first items out of the bag. She always ordered the extra-large size. You know the kind. Shaped like a bone and in an emergency, you could use four or five of them to tie down a blimp.

Dad said there had to be a hundred goodies in each biscuit bag. I don't think so. They lasted only a few days.

If Dad inadvertently bought a bag of smaller sized biscuits, Grandma would chew him out for being so careless. More than once she tried to make Dad go back to the store and get the "right" size.

When Dad commented about her feeding me so much, she'd say something like, "He's such a nice boy and he asks so politely." Dad would roll his eyes and respond with something sarcastic, like, "I bet he asks in Italian, too."

"Such short little lives our pets have to spend with us, and they spend most of it waiting for us to come home each day."

John Grogan

78

CHAPTER

20

KNOCK SMASH

Even though midday in summer could get hot in Medford, the mornings and evenings were delightful. Whenever the weather conditions were right, Grandma opened her front door a little to let the breeze flow into her apartment. When Dad saw what she was doing, he installed a screen door for her. Not only would it protect against insect intruders, but she could now keep her apartment cooler by opening the front door wider.

You know that her apartment was my second home, and I would often stop by to visit. If she didn't see me approaching, I'd knock (with either paw, I'm ambidextrous) on her screen door. Dad called it a judo chop. Because of her deafness she often didn't hear the tapping, so I'd keep it up until she spotted me.

Dad didn't object to me spending time with Grandma, but when I knocked, my paws would rip the screen. I didn't do it on purpose, it just happened. He understood the problem and bought a sheet of clear plastic at Ace Hardware and mounted it over the screen. The screen was safe.

However when I now I knocked, the door vibrated like a tuning fork and stressed the hinges. Truth is that by using my paw like an old-fashioned door knocker, I was hammering the door off its frame. Of course I thought it must be bad workmanship, cheap hinges, poor welding or whatever. But the fact was that Dad frequently needed to repair it. Eventually the screen door had to be replaced. And more than once during a single summer. Dad mumbled something about getting a discount if he bought a dozen at a time.

Grandma couldn't hear Dad cussing when he struggled to hang her door. But she thought I looked cute when I peeked over his shoulder while he worked–like I was supervising.

I have one more tidbit to tell about my visits to grandma, Of course she gave me extra treats, and Mom and Dad didn't know the half of it. Pizza, pasta, carrots, cookies, apples–and whatever other food she could dig out of her refrigerator or cupboard.

However, Mom and Dad were aware that I was getting the extra goodies at Grandma's. How else could I become the size of a hot air balloon? But not only were they concerned about my general health but didn't want excess weight adding stress to my hips.

Since they couldn't control Grandma's generosity, they reduced my mealtime food servings. I called the cutback *abuse*. Unconstitutional! Where is the ACLU when you need them? But what could I do? They claimed it was for my own good and their well-being. They didn't want a hippopotamus banging around the house.

Mom and Dad knew about Grandma's lack of canine feeding discipline for a long time. In Phoenix, she had a cute, curly haired mutt named Muffin. With Mom's prodding, she would take her dog to the vet a couple times a year for checkups. After every visit Grandma would come back with a pamphlet about canine obesity and also an attitude. How dare a mere veterinarian tell her what, and how much to feed her baby.

Tubby Muffin developed diabetes and died at the early age of eight. That was sad. She had become a good friend of mine.

"Folk will know how large your soul is,
by the way you treat a dog."

Charles F. Doran

CHAPTER

21

THE BLACKBERRY ENCOUNTER

Grandma loved to pick blackberries and during their summer growing season she'd often stroll down to the lower pasture where the bushes lined the fence. She wouldn't quit picking until she topped her stainless-steel bowl with the juicy berries. Dad asked her to tell him when she went on a picking jaunt, so he'd know her whereabouts. But being such an independent person, she ignored his requests, and I'd often hear her mutter something to him like, "I'm not a baby," or "Go wipe your nose."

Dad and I were in the barn one morning when we noticed her heading for the blackberries. "Better go with her," he said. We knew wild critters wouldn't bother her but being close to ninety and a little shaky on her feet, the risk of a fall on the uneven pasture ground concerned us.

I caught up to Grandma just as she screamed. "Snake! A snake!" She stumbled and her one-hundred-pound body teetered onto me. She half-leaned and half-sat on my back for just a few seconds, but long enough for her to regain her balance. I had saved her from falling. And maybe breaking her hip.

Now standing at my side, trying to catch her breath, she rested her hand on my head as if I were a cane. She smiled at me, and I could see tears in her eyes. "Oh, my big boy."

Dad had heard her shout and ran toward us. He saw the rescue. That's what he called it when he told Mom. "He positioned himself like a fireman catching a woman falling from a window of a building."

Mom hugged me. "My hero."

From then on Dad made her promise to take a walking stick with her to the blackberry bushes and with me as an escort. He thought that if something happened and I couldn't assist her, I could run for help.

Truthfully, I had two reasons to accompany Grandma. The first was to be her bodyguard, and the second the blackberries. She'd make a game out of it. "One for my Chase, one for the bowl. One for the bowl and two for my boy."

Hey, I was family, but doesn't everyone get paid for performing lifeguard duty, grandma sitting, or whatever they called my companion service?

Mom always knew when Grandma and I were in the pasture because I'd show up with a sooty-black tongue. And maybe a little darker muzzle too. She would accuse me of hiding the gray hairs that sprinkled my chin. I hadn't thought about that. But I could live with a Clark Gable mustache.

After the first incident, nothing ever happened on her blackberry picking outings. But I shouldn't say nothing, because her blackberry cobbler was something. Something yummy.

However, the blackberry bush invasion in the lower pasture had overwhelmed its southeast corner. Think Amazon jungle. They crushed the original five-foot wire fencing to a lamb's level. And when Mom worked the BCs with the sheep, the woolies would sometimes get tangled in the thorny tentacles.

Mom and Dad decided to attack the vines. While they marched to the pasture ready to whack the intruders, the sky darkened with ominous rain clouds. Of course, I went along to supervise. I followed while they used their loppers to cut the vines, and then about halfway a small tunnel appeared in the overgrowth. As chief of security, I deemed it necessary to investigate. I didn't want Mom and Dad attacked by a vicious animal.

I squirmed through the maze and found myself at the creek that flowed through our neighbor's peach orchard. Mom and Dad were out of sight, but I heard them hollering for me. Dad finally said, "He'll be right back."

I planned to check out the scene and hustle back to my supervising. But the scent of some strange creature singed my nose. And I saw it! Glaring at me from the side of the stream stood a brownish four-legged thing. It looked furry and about the size of a raccoon. Nothing to be concerned about because I was about three or four times the size of the critter. Just in case, I shot up my hackles into the extra-high position and made like a bear. I hounded up to this creature and in two seconds, I was a breathing pin cushion. My nose looked like a pine tree!

My howling must have sounded like a convoy of police cars with sirens wailing as I scampered back through the opening. Dad saw my muzzle and his face turned white. With Mom's help, he rushed me into the house. He checked me out while Mom hustled to gather the surgical tools necessary for my operation.

"It's a good thing the porcupine got you before you tried to bite it, or you'd have a mouthful of quills," Dad said. "Looks like you only have ten or so stuck in your nose and muzzle."

Ten? Where did he go to school? And learn to count? That critter must have shot me with a million needles!

Mom held me while Dad used a pair of tweezers to extract the quills. After he pulled the last one, Mom dabbed my nose with Bactine and, all in all, I survived. The experience was more embarrassing than painful.

After lunch we all had settled down and waited for a light drizzle to stop before we headed back to the bushwhacking. I resumed my supervisory role. Dad said, "Hey big city guy, you learning about living in the country? A critter not much bigger than an alley cat ran you off like a scared rabbit."

He was teasing, but he made me angry. So, I quit my supervising job. No two-week notice. I found a cool spot under a big oak tree to take an afternoon nap, but just as I settled down, it happened. The breeze funneled a familiar smell right between my eyes. My big nose couldn't miss it. I leaped to my feet and scooted through the tunnel. Dad shouted at me. Mom bellowed. I scurried to the creek.

And we were face-to-face again. An opportunity for revenge.

The next thing I remembered, I was up at the house and Dad had tweezers in his hand. Extracting quills. Real embarrassing.

Mom and Dad kept checking my face for several days afterward and kept applying medication. They worried about me having a reaction like I had the year before. A bumble bee had stung my cheek and my face swelled up like a pumpkin. On that occasion when I ran to Dad to show him my face, I thought he'd faint. The trip to the vet's office turned out to be the scariest episode of that day. Having a police escort wouldn't have helped–they couldn't have driven as fast as Dad did.

"In order to really enjoy a dog, one doesn't merely try to train him to be semi-human. The point of it is to open oneself to the possibility of becoming partly a dog."

Edward Hoagland

CHAPTER

22

OCEAN FUN

Mom found good homes for Jake and Cap and were both gone now. Jake's cockiness and Cap's inability to perform well in large pastures had curbed their sheep herding success.

I mentioned how Geoff's training inconsistency drove Mom crazy, and she had stopped trying to teach him to be a competitive herding dog. However, he was still her first and favorite Border Collie. That entitled him to go along on family outings.

The sandy beaches along the Oregon coast were one of our favorite fun spots. Once Diamond, Dancer, Geoff, and I saw Mom and Dad organize their beach box of towels, brushes, and water jugs, we knew an exciting outing was on the clock. With the Subaru's back seat folded down, there was enough space for all of us. We couldn't wait to jump in.

As the crow flies, the Pacific Ocean was approximately seventy-five-miles from our house, but because we had to weave through the Klamath Mountains, the trip took about three hours. We'd head southwest into Northern California, and then after reaching highway 101 head back into Oregon and our favorite coastal recreation spots.

It got a little boring along the way and we all tried to nap. But I'd often spice up the trip. From the day I arrived in the household, Diamond would harass me for reasons I still don't understand. Since all of the four leggers were in the back of the Subaru, I thought now was a good time for a little payback. As she napped, I'd nudge her. Disturbed, Diamond would snarl and click her teeth, sounding like a typewriter. It led to one of her barking conniptions. Not only did I invade her highness' space, but I had the audacity to touch her.

When Mom turned to check on the commotion, I'd be curled up with my eyes closed. But Diamond's loud animation had made her look and sound rabid. "Diamond, stop that," Mom would demand.

After Diamond relaxed, I'd take a take a short nap. Waking up, I'd casually drape a leg on her back. The commotion would start all over again. She'd get blamed each time. But other times when we were all trying to nap, I'd be gracious enough let her use my body as her pillow.

We normally arrived at the first beach communities around lunchtime. That meant McDonald's! We'd go through the drive-in and Dad would order two chicken sandwiches for Mom and himself, and four hamburgers. "But hold the buns and everything else on the burgers."

The person at the window would always question the order. "Would you please repeat that sir?" Then four long noses would appear and the kid would break into a huge smile.

The place reminded me of our bank's drive-in window. The first time I went along with Mom, the lady teller smiled and said hello. To get a better look at the cutie I stuck my head out the window. When they finished the banking transaction, Mom reached for her receipt, and I got a whiff of more than paper and ink. A dog biscuit. The teller had slipped Mom a treat for me. We pulled out and as I munched, the lady waved good-bye to me. What a place, Mom made a deposit and I made a withdrawal.

I went to the bank with Mom many times after that, and before her Toyota rolled to a stop, my head appeared with a starved look chiseled on my face. One time a new teller saw me, and her mouth flopped open. "Oh, my poor baby," she cried. Before she said a word to Mom, the young lady had three biscuits in the tray.

Because of my pleading look I thought the teller might hit her alarm button and report Mom for canine abuse. Police sirens screaming and tires screeching. Black and whites—not Border Collies of course—bolting into the parking lot. After that I softened my facial expression when I went banking with Mom. I didn't want her to get into trouble.

However, the last time we drove to the bank I saw this big box loaded with buttons jammed into the building's wall. No teller. Mom said something about new technology. An automated teller machine. Hey. No way could it replace my cuties unless it dispensed treats.

After Mom completed her transaction she had her receipt, but my drooling mouth remained empty. A catastrophe! I stared at the ATM until I thought my eyes would pop out. Dad knows about ATMs, have him fix the problem, I tried to tell her.

When we got home, Mom mentioned to Dad how indignant and pathetic I looked. Nothing about submitting a missing teller report. She made me so angry I wanted to chew up her favorite shepherd's crook.

Anyhow, the McDonald's stop wasn't the trip's highlight, but the burgers sure put it near the top of the list. Harris Beach and Boardman State Park were among the first beaches on our route, but I liked Cape Blanco best. However it was farther north, and Mom and Dad knew that once we spotted the ocean, as spoiled as we were, we'd riot if we had to wait another half hour before hitting the sand.

The beaches were always clean, and best of all, we frequently had them to ourselves. We'd hustle to the trailhead and weave our way down the switchback until we reached the beach. Then sprint up and down the shoreline with the breeze in our faces and without worrying about other dogs or people. Firm wet sand at the water's edge created the perfect track to run and the wide-open spaces created an exhilarating, born free feeling.

Right away Geoff wanted to chase anything Dad tossed–driftwood, crabs, sharks. As I said before, at times I thought the guy had lost a slice of bacon from his sandwich. He was a lot faster than me, and I couldn't beat him to a stick, but I used the technique I learned by watching football games on TV with Dad. Takeaways. I'd body block him as he returned with the object, snatch it from his mouth and return it to Dad.

Geoff didn't mind my tactics because Dad would toss the stick again and again. While we ran, Diamond would follow and do her barking gig. What a pain. I wondered how far Dad could toss her. After a while, I had enough, but Geoff dogged Dad to throw it one more time. And then again.

When Geoff got too hot from all his running he'd dash into the ocean, plop, and let the waves wash over him. Not me. I'd slowly walk into the water until I stood about knee high, and then back out. I learned from the Discovery Channel that great white sharks are the most cunning of ocean predators, so I was alert for gray-black fins, and the flash of two-inch-long teeth.

Then Dad reminded me that the water was probably too cold for them—except the fifteen footers who made exceptions for bite-size canines. Thanks, Dad. But I could see that he was watching us and wouldn't let us drift too far out into the water. More than once he mentioned something about rip currents.

Mom followed along and took pictures of us, the scenery and the unique pieces of driftwood that had washed ashore. Suddenly she stiffened and pointed to the water. "There's something out there heading for shore," she shouted.

"What is it?"

"Could be a fin."

Geoff lay in only a foot of water, but Dad grabbed him by his collar and ushered him back to the beach.

While Geoff stood aside shaking himself, the rest of us were watching the black thing moving toward us. Dad jumped up a few times trying to get a better look at the incoming object. Then he laughed. "Our sea monster is another piece of driftwood."

The four-foot log floated onto the sand sporting a small branch as its mast.

Still wary and mindful of cunning sharks I approached it. Slowly. One paw then another.

"Boo," shouted Mom.

I jumped higher than Dad did.

While the humans were laughing, Diamond pranced up to me

and with twinkling eyes, and for one of the few times in her life, she smiled.

Mom and Dad began to stroll along the beach knowing we'd follow. They watched over us as we explored, chased one another and just enjoyed the wide open spaces. After a while they turned back, ending our day at the beach.

However, before we got into the car we had to be brushed and wiped. You know how wet sand clings. And it's a problem for the thick-coated Shelties. Dancer and Diamond hated the brushing, and squirmed in misery when Mom would towel them.

The ride back always seemed shorter. Probably because we slept most of the way, in spite of Geoff's disturbing grunts while he'd dream. He must have been replaying his fun at the beach.

At home, we all got hosed down; not because of the sand but if the ocean salt water dried on our skin, we could get itchy. I didn't mind the washing, but the girls hated it, and of course Geoff loved chasing the hose spray.

"It is man's sympathy with all creatures that first makes him truly a man. Until he extends his circle of compassion to all living things, man will not himself find peace."

Albert Schweitzer

CHAPTER

23

HARVEST TIME

Mom did her dog training in the back pasture during the spring and summer. By abandoning the front pasture, it allowed the hay to grow and ensured we'd get a good crop. In a normal year we'd harvest about sixty bales. That would be enough to feed the dozen or so sheep for several months during the non-growing season. Mom would then buy whatever additional bales were needed from local farmers.

Our first crop of hay was about three feet high and ready to be cut. I had no idea of how Mom and Dad would do it, but I was sure it wouldn't be done with scissors. When sitting on the lawn on a Monday morning I heard a strange rumbling along the road and heading toward our house. Then I saw our neighbor Bill, navigate his old Ford tractor with a huge mower in tow down our driveway and into the pasture.

Once he started cutting, the tractor-mower combo whined and snorted, sounding like an angry elephant. I tried to bark. My growl became a whimper. With my tail tucked between my legs, I dashed for the barn.

Mom witnessed my reaction and ran to my side. With my back

pressed against the wall I felt myself shivering. Wrapping an arm around me she realized that the strange noises had freaked me out. "It's okay," she said. "Nothing to worry about. It's just a huge lawn mower. We'll go to the fence and watch." We stood at the gate for a minute or two, and after seeing what was going on I calmed down.

"Bill will be in and out of the pasture with his tractor for the next few days cutting and baling the hay. So, you must stay out of there. He doesn't even want Dad or me in there while he's working. It could be dangerous."

My face would have been red if I were human. But Mom took me into the house and gave me a treat. I was supposed to the tough security guy but in front of that huge mechanical monster I had become a bowl of Jell-O. Mom understood. She said, "That's exactly how humans would react if they saw a dinosaur prowling on their street." Then she rubbed my ears.

Cutting and baling the hay turned out to be a three-step process. Bill methodically drove the tractor and mower in parallel lines across the field to cut the hay. When he finished, the pasture looked like a huge, padded floor. He returned later with another piece of equipment and raked the hay into wide rows so it could dry.

When the hay had sunbathed for several days, Bill reappeared towing another odd-looking machine. I called it a mechanical buffalo. A buffalo? Well, the contraption was huge and by any standard, ugly. It would creep along each row and gobble the hay. Then creating a loud kerplunk sound, out plopped a cord-wrapped bale from its rear. Enough said?

Diamond, Dancer, and Geoff had remained in the house during the hay cutting and baling experience. I guess they suffered the same fright from the strange machines as I did. But after my initial shock, I quietly sat at the gate and watched Bill and his noisy equipment perform their tasks.

After the baling, and Bill had gone, Mom drove her pickup into the pasture. Then as she maneuvered up one row and down another, Dad loaded the bales into the truck bed. That took a while. Not because the rutted pasture required slow driving, but Dad got pooped and kept calling time out.

They wouldn't let me in the pasture while they were working, so I sat at the gate and watched.

I've mentioned our barn a few times but never described it. It was approximately the width of a five-car garage and about two cars deep. It faced the front pasture. Dad's workshop occupied one side, and the second and larger part was dedicated to the sheep.

The sheep's side of the barn had two sections. The back section housed the sheep and had water and food troughs. A six-foot high partition separated it from the front part that was open and used for storing the baled hay.

Once Mom and Dad loaded the Toyota with a manageable load, Mom backed it into the open area of the barn. They worked as a team to unload. Mom would jam a hook into one side of a bale and Dad the other, and together they would lift it off the pickup. With a floor of pallets in place, they laid a base of six bales wide and four deep. Then they stacked a row four bales high along the partition. Then a row of three and finally two, until they created a stair-step storage area.

One of the neighbors happened to stop by and Mom explained the reason for stacking the hay the way they did. "Durin the winter months and it was time to feed the sheep, we climb to the top row, tear hay from the bales and drop it over the partition into the troughs below. And the sheep munch away. Once the top two rows that are gone, we toss the hay through shuttered windows that are in the partition."

The neighbor lady smiled. "Work smarter, not harder."

However the hay encouraged field mice to spend more time in the barn. So, to defend against what Mom called an infestation, she went on the attack. Within days two male, four-month-old Manx kittens showed up. They were around for a short time, and then they were gone. Mom had shuttled the kitties to the vet's office to be neutered. And she was right to do it. A female cat can produce three litters a year and four to six kittens per litter. Do the math for a seven-year period. That's right. It could reach into the thousands!

Mom said since the cats worked at a Border Collie establishment they would have BC names. (Generally short, crisp names to be distinguishable from the shepherds' commands) She named them Moss and Toss

As planned, the cats lurked around the barn and ambushed the rodents. On occasion they'd venture into a pasture to practice their predatory technique. As long as Moss and Toss didn't come into the house, I didn't care. But they had become anti-social and would run when Mom or Dad approached them. He had installed a shelf to place dry cat food for the twins whenever they wanted a snack. But when I saw them sniffing around, I'd give them an opportunity to practice their running techniques.

Dad and I were hanging out on the deck one evening when commotion erupted from the Border Collies. Yelping and growling. Then I heard it. Strange sounds coming from the barn. I ran to investigate with Dad right behind me. We discovered a problem of having the felines around.

An adult racoon with three or four young ones, attracted by the cat food stood on the top row of baled hay. As soon as she spotted me, she hissed and snarled. A challenge. I jumped on a bale of hay two rows below her. Dad shouted. "No Chase. Dammit no!" He grabbed my tail as I lunged for the critter. "No!" He pulled and I slid back to the bottom row. I glanced up and the racoons were gone.

He put his arm around me. We both were breathing hard. "I'm sorry. But those animals are vicious when protecting their young. Their claws are like knives. Rip you into strips. Like spaghetti." I pictured a plate of Grandma's spaghetti floating in bright red tomato sauce. My blood.

The masked critters would occasionally sneak in to see if free meals were still being served. When I made my morning rounds I'd check on them and found that they usually came from the peach orchard on the east side. The experience kept my hounding skills in shape, but I guess the confrontation showed that the mother raccoon wasn't afraid of me. It deflated my ego.

Ego aside, no way I'm volunteering to sleep under the stars and stalk marauding raccoons.

"The average dog is nicer than the average person."

Andrew A. Rooney

CHAPTER

24

PEACOCK SPLENDOR

In all modesty, I'm a pretty good-looking guy. Tall, and with a beautiful golden coat. However, I couldn't match the peacocks! You know the huge flamboyant birds. When the males unveil their striking blue-green tail feathers that appear as shimmering yet intimidating eyes, they are stunning.

The birds roamed throughout our valley, and none of the neighbors knew how or when they got here. Maybe years ago the exotic creatures were kept as pets, escaped and just stayed in the area. Occasionally they wandered around our farm and made their presence known by their pooping. Big deposits, including on the roof of our house.

Mostly they perched on our deck railing, spread their wings, and flaunted their uniqueness. The feathers looked like rich satin and their green luster more gorgeous than anything that sprouted from the ground. I don't want to sound like an old romantic, but splendor they had. And when the males spread their feathers, it was nature at its regal best.

Peacocks looked like ostriches when they lumbered across the pastures. They rarely flew, but they could when threatened. When

I thought Mom nor Dad were not watching, I'd have a little fun. Just jog toward them as if I wanted lunch. And when I'd get about twenty-five feet from their tail feathers, they'd lift off, smooth as an airplane.

Dad never said it, but he didn't want me to catch one. I think after he saw my first pursuit of the birds, he knew they were safe. And that meant I was safe too because he said they were nasty when cornered.

Seeing them sway on top of a forty-foot pine tree was special though. They were the perfect Christmas tree ornament.

***

It was dinnertime on a late August afternoon with dishes of pot roast, corn on the cob and mashed potatoes decorating our dining room table. A lettuce blend salad wasted some of the space. I'd rather eat a platter of beets than that grassy stuff. I'm not a sheep.

Napkins and forks on the left of the plates and knives and spoons on the right. Each item in its proper place, including me strategically located midway between Mom and Dad's chairs.

While the Shelties parked under the table, Geoff lounged in the family room. I wanted to scratch my head about how a canine brother could ignore the highlight of the day.

Mom and Dad were talking about Laura, who had now completed her third year of college. She had decided to travel and see the United States before she finished her schooling and settle down. "I understand her thinking," said Dad, "I just hope she'll finish. It's too easy to distracted, like getting married, and never get her degree."

"I agree. But sometimes it's best to get the wanderlust out of your system before you settle down, and not regret it for the rest of your life."

Dad smiled and nodded. He had that I love you look in his eyes. He had told me he thought she was beautiful, inside and out. I'm not sure what that meant, but she was beautiful in how she treated me.

Then the peacock showed up. Bad timing. With the hubbub of Santa's reindeer crashing on the roof, a peacock landed on the porch railing. The Shelties erupted. Everyone hustled to the dining room window to see what the commotion was about. As if knowing he had an audience, the bird turned and fanned his tail feathers for Mom and Dad to gape and awe. After a minute or so of watching the creature showboat, Dad said, "Someone better move him out before he messes up the porch."

Dancer ranted as she stood at the door, so Dad opened it and encouraged her out. She took two steps toward the bird and he fluttered his wings. He gave her an evil eye, and she scooted in the house before Dad could close the door. I moved closer to the pot roast.

Dad giggled as he signaled to Diamond. "Okay big mouth, chase him away." She hesitated, slid outside, and moved toward the peacock as if the deck was a bed of hot coals. The bird wavered on the rail and flapped his wings for balance. In the time it took to say T-bone steak, Diamond ran to Mom's side.

No more delegation. It was time for the chief of household security to act. Clark Kent would have headed for the phone booth, but I eyed the source of the aroma and conjured my wrinkled-forehead, poor me expression. Dad saw my dilemma. "The pot roast isn't going to fly away but make sure that bird does."

I marched outside, my head as high as the railing. The peacock's body language telegraphed that he visualized one of his drumsticks clamped in my mouth. Excuse the pun, but he had a birds-eye view of me slinking toward him. I growled. He spun from the rail onto the lawn behind him. I ran from the porch and jogged toward him as he made runway speed to lift off. The big guy cleared the fence and in ten seconds I was back in the house.

"Good boy," Mom and Dad said upon my triumphant reentry. Diamond and Dancer pouted and muttered something about how they could have done it too. Geoff still hadn't left his spot in the family room.

I took a lap around the table and checked the plates. Because of the bird watching, no one had eaten a bite. Mom and Dad settled in their chairs, and I resumed my strategic position. I glanced toward the kitchen counter to check on the apple pie. It was still there.

Dad said, "Good job, Chase." Obviously, he was pleased with me. Maybe that meant a large bite of the pot roast. I scooted a little closer to him.

"No man can be condemned for owning a dog.
As long as he has a dog, he has a friend; and the poorer he gets,
the better friend he has."

Will Rogers

CHAPTER

25

TULIPS

Diamond lived a good life, but she always complained about something. Especially me. It seemed as if she barked at me whether I was asleep or awake, sat or stood, rain or shine. Yet, at the end I felt sorry for her.

She had recently celebrated her thirteenth birthday and her rear legs had stopped working. The vet said she had a pinched spinal cord and the nerves that controlled her legs had withered. He thought it was a congenital issue and nothing could be done for her. Diamond had to drag herself around with her front paws. Not a pretty sight.

Mom carried her outside every few hours to relieve herself.

When I'd get close to her she'd snarl, but with little vigor. Her brassy bark became a tinny grunt. Her brazen and cocky expression grew sullen, and she only wanted to be left alone. Even with all our disagreements, I had empathy for her because of my hip problems.

Even though the vet had given up on Diamond, Mom did not. She spent a lot of time on the phone and in a couple of days a huge package showed up. Dad ripped open the box and spread the contents of a two-wheel cart on the front porch. It was designed to replace Diamond's hind legs. In theory, Diamond would sit on the cart and be strapped in. Then she could propel herself with her front feet, like a human in a wheelchair.

But the wheelchair idea didn't work. Diamond didn't even try. But I did. Her cart was chest high for me, and I gently tried to push-start her. She resisted and just stood there as if Dad had loaded the cart with a ton of coal.

When Diamond performed in obedience competition, she was radiant. Everyone raved about her beauty while she sashayed around the ring. Her long golden coat and snow-white trim flowed as if she were waltzing in the halls of Versailles. Now, she looked frumpy and frail. I think, like a wrinkled movie star, she was embarrassed about her appearance and had given up on life.

Finally, Mom called the vet and asked him to come to the house and put her to rest. During the procedure Mom cradled Diamond as she had done for me when I was a sick pup. Relaxed by the gentle rocking, Diamond closed her eyes. She stirred when the needle penetrated her skin and then took her last breath. Mom sobbed as she wrapped Diamond in a pink blanket and carried her outside to her final resting place. My stomach felt queasy as Dad and I followed. His eyes were moist.

He had dug Diamond's grave under a big oak tree. It was October, and as we all watched him pat the soil, a breeze kicked up. A flurry of golden leaves, the color of Diamond's coat, rained on the site.

Dancer was the oldest of our group and I thought the most aptly named. She had a bounce to her step and was proud of herself no matter what she did. Her demeanor sparkled the most when she'd accompany Diamond on some fruitless barking expedition. After they completed their verbal assault against a swaying branch or fallen acorn, she'd prance with an expression that said don't do that again.

I liked her in spite of how she conspired against me. Looking back, it was always Diamond who instigated the harassment, and Dancer followed along to support her daughter.

The old gal was fifteen and her pace had become a slow walk. After all, that made her about eighty in human years. I remembered watching her compete in the obedience ring with Mom. They were like an Olympic ice-skating team, and their accomplishments were a source of pride for all of us.

Dancer had a happy life and peacefully passed away in her sleep not long after Diamond died. Through Dancer and their obedience training and competition, Mom met many people who became lifelong friends.

They buried her under the oak tree beside Diamond. Mom planted tulip bulbs at the site and each spring, the long-stem yellow flowers swayed at their graves. The ladies would have liked that, especially Diamond.

Geoff sat with quiet dignity at both burials. If he had a hat I know he would have held it over his heart.

The house was quiet now with the passing of the two Shetland Sheepdogs. Mom moped around the house for days, and I guess Geoff, Dad, and I did too. After an outside chore, Mom would often rest on a bale with a mug of hot coffee and invite me to sit with her. I'd plop beside her and snuggle close to remind her that she still had me. She would drape an arm around my shoulder while she drank her coffee. I loved those times. It was the perfect canine-human relationship. But not once did she offer me a sip.

"Our task must be to free ourselves
by widening our circle of compassion to embrace
all living creatures and the whole of nature and its beauty."

Albert Einstein

CHAPTER

26

APPLEGATE LAKE

As long as I took it easy when Dad and I hiked, my hips didn't bother me. Once in a while Dad would bring Geoff, and we'd sniff along the abandoned logging roads. Of course we both wanted to be the first to spot a critter, even a skunk. Fortunately, the skunk part never happened. Now that I think of it, we never caught up to any animal. That was okay with me. I didn't want any creature to get hurt. Especially if it might be me.

But I couldn't keep up with Geoff while he pursued hot scents up the hillsides. After a competitive outing with him, I would noticeably limp for a day or two afterward. That's when Dad decided that Geoff should no longer join us. But Mom made sure that he tagged along with her when she did her chores.

From March to early November, Applegate Lake became my favorite outing spot with Dad. Two streams, one from the south and the other from the west, meandered down the mountains and flowed into the beautiful lake.

The first time we visited, we stopped at the large grassy picnic area on the north shore that had ramadas and barbeque pits. At that end of the lake, a small dam controlled the water flow for the irrigation systems in the valley below.

We were walking around when we saw a blue SUV pull into the parking lot. A young man let his dog out from the back seat. After a few seconds, the dog spotted us and sprinted for me. A huge Rottweiler and wearing a muzzle cage The man screamed at his dog. Not calling it. Screaming.

As it neared, I froze. Suddenly, the dog turned and raced back as the man continued to shout. The muzzle suggested the dog had an aggression problem, but with his restraint he couldn't have caused serious harm. Still, I found myself trembling.

Dad patted me. "Don't worry we're getting out of here."

Getting back into the car, we returned to the road that ran along the far side of the lake and drove until it became a dusty single lane. We followed the dirt road for a mile or so, and as we rounded a curve we saw 14,000-foot, snow-capped, Mount Shasta poke at the sky. A stunning sight. Even at a distance it was breathtaking.

Another dirt road followed the eastern shoreline until it wandered up the mountainside and faded into a deer trail. Dad parked the Subaru near the mouth of the road, and we walked beside the lake. Tiny islands dotted the water and a fisherman in his boat waved at us.

Of course I knew how to swim, but I also knew that Dad worried about me getting hurt. Too concerned, but I think that's how most dads are. Anyhow, when I wanted a dip in the lake I'd look into his eyes, wrinkle my forehead, and then stare at the water. He understood. He'd smile, take off my leather collar, then give me an "okay."

If the lake water stood at normal depth, I could simply step in. But if low, I'd have to maneuver across a wide row of river rocks to make my entry. Either way, I'd paddle a few yards offshore while Dad walked beside me on the road. He always kept one eye on me. But if I got into trouble, he couldn't have helped me because I swam better than he did. I'd get out after a few minutes, shake the water off my coat, and we'd continue our hike. By the time we returned to the car I had dried off and Dad would slip my collar back on.

Alone with Dad, hiking along a picturesque lake with an occasional dip felt like being in heaven. Once in a while we'd get a light shower and nature would put on a display of rain droplets dancing on the lake's surface.

Dad carried a plastic water bottle, the kind that you squeeze and the water squirts out. When we'd rest, he'd unpack the bottle and show it to me. If I was thirsty, I'd sit and roll my tongue. Dad understood and squirted water into my mouth until I had enough. Then he'd give himself a few shots.

Why should he have to carry a dish and extra water for me when we could share? I saw the stuff other humans had to lug for their canines while on a hike. Back packs full of goodies, water dishes, and toys. I was embarrassed to be a dog. No consideration at all for their human friends.

**"A dog is the only thing that can mend a crack
in your broken heart."**

Judy Desmond

CHAPTER

27

DOUBLE PLAY

Mom and Dad now noticed that I had difficulty even getting onto my feather-cushioned chair-bed in Dad's study. Stepping onto it hurt my hips, and instead of enduring the pain, and unknown to them I often slept on the floor. One night Dad saw me lift a paw, whine, and back off. I must have tried it three or four times before squirming onto the chair.

The next day I found my new bed tucked into a corner of their bedroom. It was a rectangular pad with a sheepskin cover and a cotton quilt for my blanket. Of course, when I stretched out, my paws dangled over the end of the pad. Not a problem for me to sleep though. However, when the notion to complain about the pad's size crept into my brain, I'd repeat a few words to myself. Outside. Igloos. Then roll over and go back to sleep.

Mom and Dad's concern about my hips resulted in him taking me on shorter hikes and on flatter terrain. Soon our mountain treks were history. I missed all the animal smells that flowed around the mountain trails and how those experiences often made me feel like a young hound. But Dad recognized how much I enjoyed our getaways and searched for alternatives. He discovered the perfect spot. It was a lush, four-field Little League baseball complex along Bear Creek on the outskirts of Medford. And flat.

The creek flowed the year around and was bordered with trees and thick underbrush, so we knew wild critters frequented the place. A narrow dirt path ran beside the creek and behind the baseball field grass. While walking the path I had fun practicing my hounding skills. But I didn't venture into the underbrush, knowing that my body couldn't withstand an encounter.

During the off-season we had the complex to ourselves. But we were still in a much more populated area than in the mountains. If Dad spotted other people on the site with or without their dogs, on the leash I went. Not that I caused any problems, but Dad always thought you had to watch out for the other guy.

A must for Dad was a plastic bag. He stored them in the Subaru and would grab one when we got out of the car. I admit I got excited each time I saw that vast grassy area. Bottom line, I'd have to poop. I tried to wait until I got home, but if you have to go, you go. Dad faithfully waited until I finished and then picked up behind me.

The pickup routine was very important in a place like the baseball park. Imagine how a promising baseball career could suddenly come to a halt if a ten-year-old dove for a ball and gloved my...

At night critters would venture from their creek habitats and onto the baseball facilities to search for food. So that provided some fresh scents to pursue. However, Dad never let me explore the dirt infield part of the ball fields. I guess that was another rule of his. He worried that I might investigate something by digging and that would cause infield bad hops for the kids. I wasn't sure what that meant but there weren't many interesting animal smells in that area anyhow. Besides, have you ever heard of a possum playing second base? And making a double play?

"The worst sin toward our fellow creatures is not to hate them, but to be indifferent to them. That's the essence of inhumanity."

George Bernard Shaw

CHAPTER

28

A KNOCK AT THE DOOR

I'm a peaceful guy. However, that doesn't mean that my pugnacious genes don't kick in now and then. Like the day hammering erupted at the front door while Mom and Dad were having lunch. Our driveway gate had a sign nailed on it saying, **Beware of Dogs. Keep Out.** However, this character ignored it and then didn't have the courtesy to use the doorbell when he reached the house.

Startled, Mom dropped her fork. "What was that?"

I ran to the window beside the door as my deepest, meanest bark answered the sound. I planted my front feet on the sill. A man stood at the door. His eyes bugged like mushrooms when he saw my lips curled and a mouthful of teeth. I'm not sure if he got a good look because my snarling steamed the window.

Dad stepped to the door, and I pushed in front of him. No one's going to upset my family with me on duty. Dad hesitated, and then opened the door a few inches. I jumped against it and slammed it shut. He grabbed my collar and opened the door a crack and said something about it being a bad time to talk.

The man didn't run to the gate, but he moved out at the fastest walk I ever saw. He didn't bother unlatching the gate—just vaulted over it, losing his cap.

Dad snatched a napkin from the table and sponged the foam from my mouth.

"Easy," he said in a soft voice. "I've never seen you act so tough." He looked at Mom with raised eyebrows. Then he said to me, "Good boy, good boy." I calmed down.

I don't know why I acted like a crazed alligator. But the hard knock had startled me too. Maybe I got up on the wrong side of the bed, but homeland security was my job, and I always did it the best I could.

"Chase probably sensed something shady about the guy," said Mom.

She was right. I don't know what, but something more than the person's sudden appearance that set off my internal alarm. Anyhow, I would have popped my buttons, if I had any, when Dad said, "A squad of Marines couldn't provide us better protection."

I don't want to leave the impression that I ran off everyone who came to our home, because when Mom and Dad would tell me when we were having guests, I'd treat them as if they had engraved invitations from the White House. Hey, a friend of my friends was my friend too.

However, one visit got off to a slow start. Stephanie, one of Mom's college roommates and her husband Michael, lived in New Jersey, and while on west coast vacation stopped by to see us. I remember that they drove up in a big white car and it had a U.S. president's name. I know it wasn't an eight-cylinder Truman or

Hoover. Besides, Hoover makes vacuum cleaners. Maybe a Lincoln?

The relationship between human and canine aging still confuses me, but I think Mom and Stephanie were roommates about one hundred years ago.

Stephanie bounced out of the car and hugged everybody, including me. However, Michael was a no show. I stood at his door, waiting to greet him but he just peered through the half-open window. Even as I wagged my tail and threw him a smile, he continued to just stare at me. By now Mom and Dad were waiting for his exit too.

"He's harmless, Michael," said Mom.

I overheard Steph say something to Mom about "big dogs and apprehension," whatever that means.

"Back off, Chase," Dad said. I did, and the car door opened a few inches. Michael's left foot appeared, then the right. He had one eye on me as he ventured out and hugged Mom and then Dad.

I'm aware that my size makes me intimidating, especially when I stand on my hind legs, I'm eyeball to eyeball to some humans. And most don't like my paws on their shoulders, so I don't do it.

We headed for the house, and I led the way as I always did. Michael trailed and entered with one eye on me. He muttered something about dogs. "Outside. Chained," but I ignored it. I decided I was going to convert this guy into a believer of canine companionship.

After Michael and Steph hauled their stuff into the guest room, everyone headed for the family room. A large flagstone fireplace dominated the area with two large club chairs and matching hassocks placed to watch our TV. For a guy my size, I could comfortably park my butt on a hassock and watch TV with Mom or Dad. Hey, I sit on steps, chairs, hay bales, anything to make myself comfortable. They said it was part of my charm to sit like a human. Anyhow, Michael didn't know that I owned the hassocks so when he plopped on one and when I cuddled next to him, he stiffened like a Michelangelo statue. Stephanie and Mom giggled. Dad bit his lip, and Mike wanted out of there.

We sat like that for a while and as the humans talked, I walked off to get myself a drink of water. I moseyed around the house for a few minutes and returned to my seat. I sensed that Michael had relaxed a bit, and Steph said, "How cute. Pet him, Michael." His hand briefly touched me. A stroke lasted longer. After a few minutes, fingers slid up and down my back.

One more human won over. Another notch on my collar.

Mom and Stephanie had always kept in touch and exchanged Christmas cards as good friends do. Then, that December, I received a large and lumpy envelope with no return address. Mom opened it for me and pulled out a card. It was signed, *To Chase from your*

Friend, Michael. And with a Santa Claus-shaped cookie. Yep, from my amigo Michael, a dedicated card from a dedicated friend. The card was actually a picture of Mike with his other new friend, a golden lab puppy.

"The reason a dog has so many friends is that he wags his tail instead of his tongue."

Unknown Author

CHAPTER

29

THE NIGHTMARE

Mom was still looking for a Border Collie that would be a compatible herding partner. A steady, reliable performer. I heard her tell Dad, "Why can't the BCs be as dependable as Chase?" A very nice compliment, but I tried to remind Mom we don't live in a perfect world. I mean not everyone is like me.

Based on a herding friend's recommendation, Mom acquired Shep, a two-year old male, from a man in in central Oregon. He was all black except for a small white blotch of white fur on his chest, and another larger spot of white on his left shoulder. When I watched him herd sheep with Mom, I immediately thought he was too disinterested and was more suited as a family pet. In a few days I'd know if my concern was valid and he'd become another big disappointment for Mom.

My unease about Shep was right.

About a month later when grocery shopping, Mom ran into a man who she had met at trials when competing with Cap. Of course they talked about herding dogs.

Bottom line, he recommended Gem, a five-year-old female

Border Collie who had been trained by another handler and might be available. Mom called the dog's owner and arranged to see the dog perform. After watching Gem work for a few minutes Mom acquired her. She was all black with a large white bib across her chest.

After watching Gem work for a few sessions, I thought she could be a great partner for Mom. Although the smallest of all Mom's BCs, she had the most heart. I enjoyed watching them work because you could see how they clicked.

Shep and Gem would now be Mom's herding team.

Normally Mom kept twelve to fourteen sheep and separated them into two teams when she trained. That way one group would be fresh when she worked the Border Collies. However, after a while the sheep found their comfort spot with the BCs and became either defiant or too compliant.

To offset the sheep's behavior, Mom rented a ram to add fresh sheep to her flock. The man who owned the ram told Mom, "You can expect lambs in about 150 days. Normally the first birthing for a ewe will be a single lamb, and thereafter twins or even triplets."

The first lambs were so cute! A total of four, and we all fell in love with them. Especially Grandma. Mom's plan was that after the lambs were old enough to participate in the training, she would sell an equal number of the old timers. She'd be sure not to sell the ewes who had given birth until their lambs had matured.

One of the lambs had a coat as black as the others were white. While the mother ewe didn't abuse it, she wouldn't nurse it. I guess that happens until the flock realized that the black lamb was one of them. Once Mom became aware of its isolation, she began bottle feeding the little gal.

But that didn't last long! Because Grandma stepped in and took over the task. She fell in love with the sweet thing at first sight and couldn't wait for the lamb's nursing times. I don't think Mom or Dad knew, but she would warm the bottle just like a lot of human moms do for their babies. "Blackie" would be returned to the pasture after nursing so it could bed down with the flock. I thought Grandma possessed a new hop in her step and overnight had turned forty from being eighty.

Several nights later dark clouds hid the stars and created an eerie foreshadowing. When Dad and I walked outside the next morning we saw the ewes acting weird. And we didn't see the lambs. We hustled into the pasture and Dad suddenly stopped. "Oh no," he moaned. The cute fluffy lambs, days old, laid out with their stomachs ripped open. A slaughter! All the newborn. The nasty scene even made me turn away.

Since the massacre happened in the front pasture, and the BCs were kenneled at the back of the house, they didn't get wind of it. If they had heard the assault, they would have made a ruckus. That would have awakened me and I'd let Mom and Dad know we had an emergency.

Dad ran to get Mom. Tears poured from Mom's eyes as she approached the scene. Then they huddled, obviously concerned about something more than the killings. The carcasses were stacked. Strange. Coyotes wouldn't do that. Humans might. Teenagers. Maybe the killings were part of a cult. An initiation of some kind?

Dad called the Sheriff's Department.

"I've got tell my mother," Dad muttered to Mom and I saw the dread on his face. I walked at his side as we entered the apartment and found Grandma sitting on her sofa, wailing, blood stained,

118

unable to speak. She had gone out early to check on the lambs and discovered the dead. Including her baby.

"Chase, she's the one who arranged them."

Wow. How painful that must have been for her. I tried to snuggle close to her, but Grandma just placed a hand on my head for a second before it slid off. Then whined louder. Witnessing her like that hurt me more than seeing the butchered lambs.

When the deputy sheriff arrived, Dad admitted he overreacted and should not have called, but the lady officer understood. She checked the remains and confirmed that coyotes did the horrendous act.

I knew changes would be made. Mom appeared as singled-minded as I've ever seen her. She got on the phone with her herding friends and spread the story about the coyote killings. She wanted a dog with genes for the job. A K-9 commando or an ex-Green Beret.

Suggestions poured in on how to prevent another Custer massacre. This wasn't going to happen again.

"If a dog will not come to you
after having looked you in the face,
you should go home and examine your conscience."

Woodrow Wilson

CHAPTER

30

THE GUARDIAN ANGEL

A week later Mom headed for Eugene Oregon, about 150 miles north from our home. When she got back, a huge canine wearing an all-white coat jumped out of her Toyota. I gasped. I mean he was King Kong big. After all, I was used to having those twenty-pound peanuts called Shelties and the forty-pound BCs bouncing around me. Mom had already named him Gabriel.

He shook himself a few times. Then with a self-assured, wolf-like lope he circled the truck, and with steely, yellow-brown eyes checked out his new territory. It was like a scene from a Western movie when the hero steps out of a stagecoach, ready to clean up Dodge City.

When I approached him, I felt like I was peering up at the Washington Monument. He weighed in at one-ten if he weighed an ounce. Maybe he wasn't much bigger than me, but he sure demanded attention.

Grandma gushed when Mom explained that Gabriel was a Maremma, whose ancestors originated in the province of her parents in Italy. She knelt beside Gabe, gave him a long hug, and then kissed his coat. She acted as if he was the Pope. Then Mom told Grandma that the dog lives with sheep and is capable of handling wolves, one on one.

A chill hit me. Would Grandma shunt me to a sidetrack? No more visits. No more treats. My ears drooped and my forehead wrinkled like a dirty sheet.

I know the family loves me. A lot. But I guess I still carry some paranoia from being discarded as a pup. No longer wanted or needed. Fortunately, Dad read my dismay. As we sat on the porch step, he explained the situation. He went through this management lingo, like functional responsibilities and allocation of duties. Gabriel's job was to guard the sheep. A hired gun that would live with the critters. Outside. In the rain, snow and cold.

"Chase, your role is to protect Grandma, Mom, and me. Inside. Like the head of the Secret Service. With a warm house, soft bed, and a permanent job. And hey, you know that Grandma will love you forever."

Enough said. I jogged over to Gabe and welcomed him to the family.

Mom knew that the Maremma breed had a reputation for being "maternal" with sheep. Yet, she wasn't sure what to expect when she introduced Gabriel to her flock. She hooked him to a leash and slowly led him toward the woollies. To be honest, I didn't know what to expect either. If Gabe became aggressive, Mom wouldn't be able hold the big guy. Did she want me to jump in? Stop him? I didn't like how this was shaping up.

Mom unleashed Gabe and he loped toward the sheep. They remained calm. Knowing. He acted like a perfect gentleman as he scooted nose-to-nose with them, as if introducing himself. Then he stepped back and fixed his gazed on the ewes, creating the presence of the new CEO, explaining pasture policy and procedure.

When all was quiet, he'd play with the sheep and even nap with them. I know Mom, Dad, and Grandma thought it a marvelous example of nature's children coexisting. I did too, especially when the sheep would cuddle next to him and they would appear as a white blanket on a velvet green bed.

And I had no trouble sleeping knowing that Gabriel was on the job.

"Nonviolence leads to the highest ethics, which is the goal of all evolution. Until we stop harming all other living beings, we are still savages."

Thomas Edison

CHAPTER

31

BATTLE STATIONS

It was inevitable. A farmyard not big enough for two top dogs.

I stood at the gate near the barn when Gabe appeared. Without warning he leaped at my throat. His lunge knocked me into the fence. I bounced back and slammed him with my chest. Growling, he came at me again. I stymied his charge with a rush of my own. We were like Muhammad Ali and Mike Tyson duking it out.

Dad must have heard our snarls because he shouted as he ran toward us. "No! No! No! Damnit stop." He jumped between us and tried to push us apart. Then it was over. With no blood, thank goodness.

Sane humans know not to leap into the middle of a canine fight. Especially if the size of both combatants make Lassie look like a puppy. Dad knew that better than anybody. His intervention was stupid. Neither Gabe nor I would have hurt him on purpose, but things happen when combatants attempt to bite and gash their opponent.

The uproar must have sounded pretty fierce, because Mom heard it from inside the house and arrived on the scene just as the ruckus ended. "No one hurt" Dad told her. He was still breathing hard. "I jumped into the middle of their fight. Dumbest thing I've ever done."

Mom brushed off Dad's shoulder. "You can say that again." I stood there shaking. She hugged me and watched Gabe jog back to his flock. He acted like nothing had happened.

Normally I'm a peace-loving guy and turn the other cheek, but there are situations when you must defend yourself. After I thought about it, the bout could have been billed as the Wolf Destroyer versus the Lion Hunter. I guess it ended in a draw, but I was proud of how I held my own against the big guy.

Gabe and I got along okay after that. We just stayed out of each other's way. But I admit I was wary when he walked by, and I still don't know what triggered the brawl.

I didn't lobby for the Nobel Peace Prize, but one time I stepped in when Shep and carefree Gem got into it. Their face-to-face growls erupted into combat, and I threw myself between the two, wanting to save one or both of them from a ripped throat. I'm twice their size and sent both flying head over paws.

When Mom arrived at the scene, Dad met her. "I saw it all. The BCs began fighting and Chase dove between them to intervene. Shep backed off, but Gem was still angry and attacked Chase. The Big Guy's instincts just kicked in when she turned on him."

Mom ran to Gem and saw the blood on her.

I'm embarrassed to say that because of my reaction Gem ended up at the animal hospital. Thankfully nothing too serious. Except for the vet's bill, it ended okay.

As I said, I don't like to see blood. Certainly not mine, nor anybody else's. I think Dad was proud of me for breaking up the Border Collies' fight. At least I heard him tell the story several times to his friends.

"Recollect that the Almighty,
who gave the dog to be companion of our pleasures
and our toils, hath invested him with a nature noble
and incapable of deceit."

Sir Walter Scott

CHAPTER

32

DAD AND ME

If Dad didn't drive to the nearby mountains for a hike, he'd walk along the two-lane Griffin Creek road in front of our house. The shoulders were narrow with steep drop-offs into ditches often overgrown by wild blackberry bushes. Sometimes cars would speed down from the mountains and whiz by him. Therefore, when he refused to take me with him because he said it was too dangerous, I understood.

But being a worrywart, I sat at the driveway gate and watched him until he was out of sight, and then I howled. If you're on a trestle and hear a train hoot, you perk up and stay alert. And if Dad got lost, he could find his way home by tracking my voice. Besides, once I could no longer see him, I didn't know if he had been knocked into a ditch or been given a ride on some teenager's car hood.

I guess the neighbors, even though they were a long way off, knew when Dad took a walk. Sorrowful howling carried a long way in our charming valley.

You know by now that Dad and I had a special relationship, and in part, it was due to the respect he showed for me. For example, many of my canine colleagues know how to shake hands. They perform when told to "roll over," "play dead," or "sing for your supper." Humans think it's cute, but to me, so sophomoric and humiliating. Dad thought so too. He never asked me to perform in such a demeaning manner.

I'll tell you the one thing I did but *"My Way,"* as Frankie Sinatra would sing it. Dad's a big sports fan and we'd often enjoy watching football on TV, even though the celebration antics of some players turned us off. Watching the guys "chase" one another made my juices hot, and after a great play, Dad would say, "Give me five." I'd slap his hand with my paw and then he'd wrap me with a big hug.

My favorite team? Hey, the Detroit Lions. Who else could I root for with all that Ridgeback blood flowing through my veins?

The one expression Dad appeared to overlook in our relationship was my smile. Like when the corners of your mouth curve upward and you display your teeth. For me, that meant my conical pointed teeth situated between my lateral incisor and first premolar. One dictionary says, "people smile when they are pleased, amused or when they are being friendly." Webster's Dictionary adds the words "eyes brighten."

When Dad drove off on an errand and I wasn't able to join him, I'd wait at the driveway gate to greet him when he came home. He would stop the car at the gate. Open it, drive through, stop, and get out again. Then he'd latch the gate behind him. A laborious process, but it kept the canines from taking off and exploring the valley on their own.

Before he got back in the car to drive it into the garage, he'd give me a big hug. I would beam to show that I was happy to see him. I mean the bigger the mouth, the bigger the smile. Right? No one could miss it—except Dad.

With Mom's puppy school, obedience competitions and herding, she'd seen hundreds of canines, and she knew a smiler when she saw one. It was Mom who mentioned it to him one day when they came home from shopping.

"You've never commented on Chase's smile," she told him. It sounded like an admonishment. I didn't want to get him in trouble, but Mom was right. He'd never said a word about it.

Dad rubbed my ears. "I noticed his smile years ago. I guess I took it for granted." He patted my back. "Sorry, big guy, I've always appreciated your greeting."

The acknowledgment, albeit years late, made me feel good. At least it wasn't posthumously.

For the record, I heard Mom say that smiling is not a common canine behavior. Although some dogs maybe do it to imitate humans, the gesture often gets misinterpreted. I guess most of my peers figured that flashing their snowy whites fangs when meeting humans was often interpreted as an antisocial greeting.

"If the kindest souls were rewarded with the longest lives, dogs would outlive us all."

Unknown Author

CHAPTER

33

GABE THE GREAT

I had a free pass to wander around the farm, and that enabled me to observe my canine associates. I made mental notes about the smart things I saw them do. All in all, I think the Border Collies are the most intelligent I've been around. They appeared to learn the commands in a day or two, and their genes enabled them without much hesitation to anticipate the sheep's movements. It must be their British Isles heritage where the crisp, cool weather stimulated their brain cells.

But what happened to their neighbors, the Shetland Islanders? Some of the Shelties' brains must have mutated into extra-large vocal cords. However, I'm probably too harsh on the Shelties because although their herding skills were nil, their obedience ring performances were magnificent.

But intelligent canine brains must have flourished in Gabriel's Italy too. I must tell you how I saw him perform his duties on more than one occasion—like an air raid warden reacting to sirens. If he heard an unusual sound or got a whiff of a strange smell, he'd evaluate the risk and if threatening, he shepherded the sheep toward the safe end of the pasture. Or even into the barn. Then he'd dash to the fence line where the predator may be lurking.

Ready for battle. Very impressive. A real pro.

And I saw the result of one of his encounters with coyotes when they thought they'd get another free dinner.

After the slaughter of the lambs a while back, the ram visited again and several months later we had another birthing. Three cuties were with the ewes in the rear pasture, which is adjacent to the kenneled Border Collies.

One night after darkness had settled in and I had gone to bed, coyote howls echoed throughout our valley. Not unusual, as they often roamed at night. And so without concern I fell asleep. It was after midnight when the Border Collies' loud barking woke us up. Dad rushed outside waving a flashlight. I followed him. By the time we got to the back pasture the furor had ended.

Dad swept the flashlight's beam across the area. The ewes were gone. And the lambs too. We saw only Gabe standing with his paws on top of the back fence, howling into the blackness.

We jogged toward him. Then Dad shouted, "Hold it," and he pivoted toward the barn. I heard it too. A stirring. Slowly approaching the door, he flashed his light inside. The frightened ewes huddled in a corner.

"My God, Chase. They're all in here. The lambs too."

Then Gabe joined us. "Damn! You've got blood all over your coat." On his knees, Dad grabbed him around his neck and checked for wounds. "That must be coyote blood."

The barn lights flashed on, and Mom stood at the doorway.

"I don't know how he did it, Marianne, but he got all the sheep in here, and still must have injured some of the damn coyotes."

Mom snatched the flashlight from Dad and inspected her flock. "I don't see a drop of blood on any of them." She hugged Gabe, didn't say a word. But I saw tears stream across her cheeks.

The next morning Mom checked the sheep one by one. They were all injury free. We went into the pasture to search for evidence of a fight. As we neared the fence, I spotted two small tufts of fur on the grass.

"They're from a coyote," said Dad. Then he noticed digging under the fence. "That's how the coyotes entered and left the area. There had to be at least two of them, maybe four or five, but Gabriel clearly won the battle."

Remember, a Maremma was bred to fight wolves, so his size and fierceness were enough to discourage a band of coyotes. And that night he proved it.

Another tale about Gabe has to do with the peacocks.

Often I'd sit under the oak trees at the fence line and watch Mom and the BCs work the sheep. During the hot summer, she trained in the morning while Gabe parked in a shady, remote spot to catch up on his sleep. Remember, he worked the night shift, because that's when the predators prowled.

This one July morning, a handful of peacocks fluttered into the pasture. Not unusual and they kept their distance from the sheep and were not a training distraction. Today was no different, but Shep was making it tough for Mom. He scrambled the sheep like an omelet, not paying any attention to her commands and just screwing up. But I knew he hadn't slept well. Had a nightmare about missing breakfast and therefore got up on the wrong side of his igloo.

Mom's eyeballs hid in dark slits, and her cuss words singed my tail. You could have fried a pork chop on her forehead. She whipped off her Aussie hat and at the same time spied the birds. Although they were faultless, Mom decided they were the blame for Shep playing demolition derby with the sheep. She attempted to shoo them away, but the omnivores scooted a few yards and continued their search for snacks in the pasture grass.

Then Mom spotted Gabe dozing in one of his cool, shallow foxholes he had dug for himself. Both eyes were closed but one ear and one nostril were on high alert. Trust me. The Big Guy knew what was going on. "Get those damn birds out of here," Mom shouted at him. He opened one eye, and then the other, but didn't move a paw.

The sheep, Shep, peacocks, and now Gabe had tweaked Mom's nose. She slammed her crook down and headed for the gate. I greeted her, but she rushed by me with Shep at her side and deposited him into his kennel.

When she hooked the latch, I parked against her leg. Of course, Mom couldn't resist me. She knelt and gave me a big hug. "Good boy," she said. "Good boy." With her arms locked around me I sensed the tension flow out of her like air from a balloon.

Who needs Aleve or Tylenol when I'm around?

A couple of days later Mom invited a herding friend over to observe her work with Shep. The lady was an experienced trainer and after watching for a while, told Mom that she thought Shep had potential, and she would be willing to work with him. I saw them talk for a few minutes, and then the lady left with Shep. Mom had given him to her friend.

Later I overheard Mom and Dad discussing Shep, and she had

concluded that for whatever the reason, they were just not a compatible team. My heart ached for Mom. I knew how hard she tried to get him to respect her but I saw that their relationship never clicked. For now, Gem would be her only working dog.

Anyhow, back to Gabe and the peacocks. He got up from his foxhole, shook himself, glanced at the birds and moseyed toward the sheep. He drifted among them as if saying good morning and asking if they had a hardy breakfast.

Then he focused on the peacocks, as if thinking you gotta do what you gotta do and loped toward them. He looked serious and the birds were confused. They had entered the pasture dozens of times, and he had looked the other way. He knew they weren't a threat to his flock, but he had his orders and the peacocks sensed it. They were up, up and away.

Gabe understood that Mom wanted the birds out of the pasture, so after that he kept them away. No more visiting rights.

I've got one more story to tell about the Big Guy. He had now been with us for over a year and during his tenure, several lamb litters were born without one loss, even while coyotes lingered nearby. As a canine, I was proud of his record.

But Gabe was head-over-heels in love with a fuzzy ewe. Every morning he ran to her and licked her muzzle. When he kissed her, his tail looked like a flag in a hurricane, and the ewe's stubby tail gyrated as feverishly as his did.

When winter rolled around, Mom tossed hay in the barn feeders at mealtime, but only one ewe, Gabriel's girlfriend, entered the building. She sauntered in as if she was Miss America, and then gorged herself. He blocked the door until his gal ate her fill. Once she ambled out, he allowed the flock to enter and attack the leftovers.

Every guy needs a gal. I understand that, and neither he nor I could ever have kids. However, as the cop on his beat, he had to be objective and not show favoritism. And I never saw such a blatant display of unfairness. I thought discrimination laws stopped things like that.

But the Favored One had turned into a wide-bodied ewe. The ram for rent had visited months ago, so was she expecting or only fat? The image of her delivering fluffy white puppies flashed through my mind.

I didn't know if I was watching a rerun of Desperate Housewives or Peyton Place. And I didn't know how Gabe would cater to the ewe's babies. Would he file for adoption?

Finally, the hippopotamus look-a-like had her babies. She produced twins, cute vanilla-colored female lambs. No doubt that the father was of the sheep species, so no history made there.

When the lambs were a few days old, Gabriel approached the Favored One with his usual flirtation antics. Until then I didn't think any critter south of a Bengal tiger could make him scurry, but she ran him off in a cloud of dust. The romance? Dead. Gone, like a slice of baloney in my mouth.

She had used him to get special privileges. I guess guys can't trust some gals. However, as the lambs grew, she allowed her babies to play or take a snooze with the white giant. After all who would you rather have as a babysitter and bodyguard?

**"Histories are more full of examples of the fidelity
of dogs than of friends."**

Alexander Pope

CHAPTER

34

SHAZAM

How could that happen?

Mom and Dad were divorcing! It hit me like a bolt of lightning! There was no shouting or screaming like you see on Divorce Court. Not once did I sense any negative electricity between the two.

I guess they had been discussing it but without arguing. And because of my limited knowledge of the language and without any fiery dialogue from them, I had no inkling of it.

I knew for some time Mom had been feeling wistful. Agonizing over something. She spent a lot of time talking to a friend in Phoenix who was a family counselor. She met with local counselors too. They concluded Mom had been repressing her feelings for years. She was gay.

It floored Dad! Mom said she asked Dad for the divorce because once he knew, it would be an awkward marriage. She wanted him to be happy and for her to be free of her emotional struggles. I know that they cared a lot for each other because before my eyes they went from being husband and wife to brother and sister.

I loved them both and didn't want to be without either one. A weird knot lingered in my chest. I drifted for days, like being rudderless on a flying carpet. Yet, it would have been worse if I had to coexist with them screaming at each other.

I think Dad struggled with a variety of feelings. After the initial shock, he drifted through a variety of emotions. Despair and sadness, disbelief and even anger. I know he saw a counselor several times.

Mom moved out of the house, and she stopped working the Border Collies. I can't imagine how much it pained her to quit. She had sharpened her training skills, gained confidence, and had become a serious contender to win any trial she entered.

And best of all, she'd had so much fun working with the dogs and sheep and met many nice people along the way.

All her BCs had good herding genes and performed well at times, but not enough to consistently win on the trial circuit. Through the years Jake, Shep, and Cap ended up in homes where they could forego their herding credentials and be happier as companions. Gem had performed the best of all Mom's Border Collies, winning a few trials, and earned a reputation for being a reliable herder. Until she found the right home for Gem to work as a herding dog, she would keep her. Geoff was still Mom's baby boy, and he would also remain with her.

Mom and Dad chose not to tell Grandma about their divorce. They decided to say that they were going to live separately for a while, and she accepted their plan without a question. I thought it strange, but Mom and Dad weren't surprised by her reaction.

Mom moved out of our Griffin Creek home and found a temporary place in Medford that had space for her to keep Geoff and Gem. I stayed with Dad and Grandma, but I also saw Mom a lot too. She would come by to see how we were doing, spend a little with Grandma, and let her dogs run.

I watched how Mom and Dad made their personal adjustments, especially Dad, since we were joined at the hip. He just roamed around, checked on the sheep a lot and spent more time with Grandma.

When Mom and Dad's friends heard of the spilt, they were as shocked as I had been. Tom, one of Dad's former work buddies in Arizona, flew to Medford and spent several days with us. He hadn't seen Dad in years and said he wanted to visit and have a golf vacation. But I think he wanted to see how Dad was doing. I liked Tom and the two of us got along great.

I'm not sure what Tom reported to Dad's friends in Phoenix, but soon after Tom returned home, Helga showed up in Medford. She also had worked with Tom and Dad. It had been several years since Dad last saw her, and that was when he attended her husband's funeral in Phoenix. As it turned out, Mom and Dad and Helga and her husband had been longtime friends.

I could tell right away that Helga liked me. But I must admit, pretty women are just attracted to me.

"No matter how little money,
and how few possessions you own,
having a dog makes you rich."

Louis Sabin

CHAPTER

35

POOR GRANDMA

Mom had purchased a pretty condo in Ashland, Oregon with a little yard for Geoff and Gem to stretch their legs. Since she lived about twenty miles from our West Griffin Creek home, I considered her to be living in the neighborhood. She invited Dad and me over to see her layout and to have dinner. My old canine friends appeared to be happy to see me, and spending time with Mom was always a treat.

Around that time Mom was contacted by a woman in Maryland inquiring about Gem. Wow! Gem must have had quite a reputation for someone that far away to even know about her. After several conversations with the lady, Mom sent Gem to the east coast. We were all delighted about Gem being given a new opportunity.

However, when Mom told Dad that she was gone, she cried. A lot. Now it was just Geoff to keep her company.

But Grandma had become an issue. A few months before the divorce bombshell, Dad noticed how reserved she had become and just stayed in her apartment. She had always insisted on helping by doing small chores around the farm. She'd sweep the deck every day, rake leaves, pull weeds, and do a dozen other tasks.

Dad took her to the doctor, and he confirmed what we all had suspected. Dementia. She had vascular dementia which affects the brain, causes memory loss and general confusion. It was in the early stages and so the doctor suggested that Dad watch her more carefully, but to expect the worst.

When I visited grandma, she'd give me a goody, and then sit on her sofa with a glazed look in her eyes. And she wore the same clothes for days at a time and rarely cooked for herself. Then she became argumentative and stopped changing her clothes or even bathing. When Mom came by to assist Dad with Grandma's hygiene needs, that too turned out to be an argumentative struggle between the three of them.

For years, I watched Grandma start her day parked in front of her Sony TV. She loved watching the Food Channel, nose to nose with Emeril, her beloved host. However, now a war of words with him had caused a divorce.

She started shouting about Emeril as soon as Dad and I walked into her apartment. "That fart said my spaghetti sauce needed more fresh green peppers, and more garlic salt when I boiled water for cooking the pasta. I was making it while he was a baby crawling around in dirty diapers." Her era of being mesmerized by Emeril ended when she threatened to hurl a bottle of olive oil at him. I wanted to cry.

She now parked for hours on her favorite captain's chair in her bedroom. Her dull eyes stared at family pictures hanging on the wall as if wondering who those people were.

Sometimes when I sat with her it seemed as if she just looked through me. Weeks earlier she couldn't wait for me to visit her–the highlight of her day. But now I didn't exist. I wanted to shake her. Grandma, here I am!

She finally told Dad that she'd parked in the bedroom because she didn't like the TV people criticizing her. The Sony clicked off for the last time when she said some woman told her to put more sticker on her dentures. Sounds funny, yet sad for Dad and me to hear her babble like that.

Now, Dad checked on Grandma every few hours, with me going along to help if I could. She seemed contented when I sat with her, but soon she'd close her eyes and doze.

Then Grandma began telling Dad that her bedside clock woke her up every morning. Not that she minded because it played tunes of old Italian melodies. Of course he knew her claim was screwy because it was a bare-bones digital type and not a clock radio. And remember, she was so deaf that she couldn't hear a pack of howling wolves if they were sitting on her bed.

Mom and Dad had decided that for Grandma's sake they should keep her in familiar surroundings as long as they could. But now she just wandered around her apartment, lost, at risk for doing something harmful to herself. At times her behavior became contagious. After seeing her, I would meander outside, drift from fence to fence, hear nothing, and see nothing.

Dad would leave me in charge of her for short periods of time while he went into town to meet Mom. He told me they were scouting nursing homes that would care for Grandma around the clock.

However, when he drove off, he would always padlock the driveway gate. I guess Dad had visions of his mom aimlessly walking along West Griffin Creek Road with me tagging along.

After evaluating a handful of care centers, Dad arranged to place Grandma into a nursing home that provided the constant attention she needed. I was with him when he told her.

"Mom, I've found a nice apartment for you. With really nice neighbors."

"How do you know they're nice?" Then she said some bad words that I had never heard from her. I thought some awful person had taken over her body.

"You'll have ladies who will help you with the chores so you can enjoy yourself. And just take it easy."

"Bull shit. Who are you to tell me how to live my life? I'm not going anywhere."

Yeah. That's how their conversations were. We were hesitant to enter her apartment in fear of triggering another hailstorm of anger. The exchanges lasted just a few minutes, but it felt like hours to me. Probably days for Dad.

The day came to move, and Mom came by to help Dad select and pack Grandma's clothes. She sat with Mom in our house while Dad took her bed and furniture pieces to the nursing home. When Dad drove her out of our driveway for the last time, she was icy and silent. And she had not said goodbye to me. That hurt. But I understood.

Mom stayed behind to help clean Grandma's apartment and console me. Finally, she left and I was alone. Alone for the first time that I could remember, but I knew Dad would be back as soon as he had his mother settled. Everything now was quiet and peaceful, but I just roamed around the house as if I was lost in some strange land.

All families have changes for good and bad, but ours had been stable for so long I never thought this time would come. I guess we were all in the September of our years and maybe even December for some of us.

When Dad got back, he told me Grandma sat like a statue during the trip to the nursing home, but when she met the staff and her new housemates, she became talkative and sociable. However, when he gave her a peck on the cheek as he left, she gripped his arm.

"No! You can't abandon me. Not after all I've done for you! You shithead!"

The head nurse gently peeled her off him and encouraged Dad to leave, telling him it was common for new residents to behave that way.

As soon as he walked through the door at home he drifted into the living room and collapsed on the sofa, guilt streamed from his eyes. I rested my paw on his leg to console him. Dad, you still have me.

Mom stopped by the next day and told him that he made the right decision. There was no question that Grandma needed professional care. He hugged her, Mom's words made me feel better too. After she left, Dad asked me if I wanted to see Grandma in a week or so, and naturally I did. But the day before I was going to visit her, Dad received a phone call.

"Your mother tried to sneak out last night and fell. She broke her hip."

Six days at the nursing home and now in the hospital. After three weeks they transferred her into the physical rehab and convalescent home across the street from the hospital. Dad said she was angry all the time and ranting about wanting to go home. Of course, that was out of the question more so than ever.

So in about a month Grandma had experienced her third set of beds, colors, and smells as well as a cadre of new faces fussing over her. For a ninety-year-old with dementia, that's tough. That's tough for anyone.

I knew the way to the nursing home because Dad and I always drove by the place when we visited Mom. We entered the building's double security doors, and Dad signed us in. Other visitors, residents and nurses welcomed me with smiles, but all I wanted was my Grandma. After scurrying through a maze of halls we found her in bed. A floor-to-ceiling, beige curtain divided the room and provided privacy between her and her roommate.

I noticed that Dad had hung family pictures on her wall. Sitting on the nightstand was a picture of Grandma standing by a fence with me at her feet. I felt a lump in my throat.

She recognized me, patted my head a few times and drifted off to sleep. So much for me energizing her. However, while Dad and I were there, I wanted to check the place out and be sure everything was at its best for my Grandma.

Dad pointed out the amenities as I followed along. Overall, it looked nice. A spacious TV room, game room, small library, the usual stuff. I stuck my head in a few rooms to meet the guests. They appeared happy to see me, so I let them baby talk and pet me for a few minutes.

All the caregiver books say that petting dogs helps humans feel better, and I wanted to do my part. Making people smile ranks high on my resume of accomplishments.

Finally, I engineered a wrinkled forehead with an expression that asked *where is it*? Dad's cool. He knew what I meant. The most important part of the nursing home. I needed to inspect *the room*.

Dad winked at me. "I'll show you where it is."

We turned down a few hallways and I got the smells. We were getting close. Then like the Pearly Gates, it appeared. Double swinging doors but with a big red sign plastered on one of them. "Employees Only."

Dad crouched beside me. "It's not you. Everybody stays out of the kitchen unless they work in there."

I didn't like it, but I understood their silly rules. Dad let me linger a few minutes. He knew I was checking the smells. Fried chicken, I tried to tell him. I took another deep breath, mashed potatoes with a hint of garlic and giblet gravy. Tossed salad with a choice of dressing, Italian or ranch. When the aroma of a tangy peach cobbler reached my nose, I had found my heaven.

Dad said, "Chicken, potatoes with gravy and peach cobbler for dessert."

Whoa. I flipped out. I thought we had a real ESP thing going. Then I saw he was reading the menu posted on the bulletin board.

He brought me back a few weeks later, and I found Grandma in a wheelchair. She said, "Nice doggie," and rolled by. She didn't even touch me. How can she not know me? My heart fell to my stomach. I knew she wasn't well, but she had loved me so much. Her baby. Now I had become just another doggie.

Dad said, "Don't feel bad, Grandma doesn't recognize me either."

He patted my head. "I guess we better go. But do you want to check out the dinner menu first?" I gave him my "you betcha" look, and we headed for the kitchen.

***

There was nothing more Dad could do for Grandma. As the weeks passed, her memory kept regressing, and she now lived in her teenage years, well before Dad's days on earth. I know how it stung me when Grandma brushed me off, but I can't imagine what Dad thought when she didn't know who he was. I guess that happens a lot when family members get dementia.

Mom and Dad had a long talk about Grandma. They were concerned about her long-term care and wanted to make sure she had quality attention. I cared too.

The convalescent home, which also had a memory care wing, became her permanent home.

**"You think dogs will not be in heaven? I tell you,
Othey will be there long before any of us."**

Robert Louis Stevenson

CHAPTER

36

RESTLESS GABE

Since Mom had stopped her Border Collie training, the flock just munched all day, living like queens. At the same time, the predators in the area had spread the word to stay away from the white Maremma and his ewes. So Gabe often entertained himself by figuring out how to circumvent the fencing and explore the neighborhood. It became an ongoing chess match between canine and human. Dad would secure all possible escape routes, yet an hour later there was Gabriel strolling through the peach orchard next door.

"Damn him. How did he do that? Chase, he's your buddy you must know."

Dad's a good human and all that but watching my canine associate outsmart him made me smile.

Gabriel had figured out that the obstruction in the irrigation ditch at the fence line was a swing gate. Not fixed. When we received irrigation, the flowing water swung open the gate but otherwise it remained in the down or "closed" position. In theory, the pseudo barrier provided security for keeping predators out and the sheep in. So when Gabe wanted out of the pasture when

146

no water flowed in the ditch, he'd jump in, push the gate toward the orchard, squirm through and let it swing closed behind him. Free and ready to explore.

I saw that Gabriel was restless and had outgrown his responsibilities on our small farm. He needed a bigger challenge. He needed a promotion. Fortunately for Gabe, Mom saw it too. She told her sheep owner friends that Gabriel was available if the right opportunity for him came along.

A security position opened when a sheep rancher about one hundred miles north, near Roseburg, Oregon, needed a coyote solution. Mom took Gabriel to meet the rancher and take a look at the farm. That was the last time I saw him. The Roseburg rancher liked Gabe, and the opportunity to protect scores of sheep across acres of rolling hills was a challenge the Big Guy readily accepted.

I missed him even though we didn't always see eye to eye. But unlike most of Mom's pedigree Border Collies who weren't successful trial dogs he exceeded all expectations. He could be ferocious toward predators and yet gentle as the lambs he safeguarded.

Mom put an ad in the newspaper to sell the sheep. A couple of days later a guy responded, and Mom and I met him at the gate. He wore a dirty camouflage cap and an unkempt reddish beard. My instincts screamed "look out" about this guy. The creep told Mom he wanted to expand his flock.

He spent some time inspecting the sheep, but when talking to Mom he never stopped looking at the ground. Acted as if he was afraid of stepping into a manhole. I kept circling him, growling, telling Mom in my own way that I suspected he was a bad hombre.

"Chase. Stop that," Mom hollered. I did. I backed off a few feet and sat, still growling.

He offered to buy all fifteen head.

When he left, I followed him to the gate. I sensed his discomfort. Maybe it was fear. As he closed the gate, he swore at me and jumped into his truck.

Mom sold the flock to him, and it turned out the guy never paid her. I tried to warn her that he wasn't trustworthy. Did everything I could, short of biting his leg.

Mom checked on Gabe from time to time, and the Roseburg lady said he had a great record. No losses, increased sheep morale and a 100 percent approval rating from the flock.

A younger guardian dog named Joseph also worked on the ranch. Gabe showed that he could be a dog trainer too, because we heard that whenever the kid did something stupid around the sheep, he'd flatten him.

However the last time Mom inquired about him, the lady choked up. She struggled to explain that they found him surrounded by the sheep as if he could still protect them. He died from natural causes.

**"May I always be the kind of person
that my dog thinks I am."**

Unknown Author

CHAPTER

37

SLOW, SLOWER, SLOWEST

I felt as if needles were stuck into my hip and the pain made my gait look like an awkward shuffle. When Dad took me to see Dr. Dale, he mentioned not only my hips but how lethargic I had become. After a discussion, the doctor recommended that I stop the Rimadyl thinking that it could be causing my sluggishness, and to replace it with oxycodone, a narcotic painkiller.

The new pill helped, but after four or five hours the full effect of the drug wore off. However, I appreciated the temporary relief it gave me.

Dr. Dale advised Dad that he stop all our outings. That was okay because even though I would miss the change of scenery, I had enough space around our small farm to roam. And even climbing in and out of the Subaru had become too much for me. Dad had attempted to help by lifting me in, but he couldn't stand my cry of pain that often accompanied the effort. He even built me a ramp with a gentle incline to make it easier to get in. Nothing worked. My trips in the car would be limited to only the vet's office.

But would the cost of my medical care be too much for Dad to bear? My fear of going back to the animal shelter again resurfaced.

Insecurity dwells deep within most adopted canines who had spent time jailed in cages. I was no exception and because of my physical condition I would no longer be adoptable.

I still wondered why I ended up at the Humane Society kennels to start with. Obviously, I wasn't wanted. But why? What did I do?

What about my siblings? Where were they? Victims of uncaring humans who discard the unwanted? In the bathtub like many puppies and kittens? It happens. I've overheard workers at the kennels talk about it. I was actually one of the lucky ones.

Then Sunday morning I awoke with a feeling of euphoria with a vision of a pure gold chain linking the hearts of Mom and Dad to mine. The revelation had made clear the absurdity of my anxiety. My human parents loved me as much as I loved them. How could I ever have doubted that?

After breakfast I moseyed to Dad's side. He sat comfortably reading the newspaper. I tapped his leg.

"What's up? You've just eaten," he said.

I love you, I tried to convey to him. He smiled and caressed my ears. I plopped to the floor and rested my head on his foot.

While Dr. Dale continued his practice in Talent, he opened another office in Medford and hired Dr. Steve to run it. We started visiting the Medford office because it was much closer to home.

I liked Dr. Dale, but Dr. Steve made me feel as if I was his sole patient. And I liked the way he rubbed my ears when he discussed my medical conditions with us. Anyhow, he became my primary care provider.

Weariness continued to consume me, and Dr. Steve knew it was from the medications' side effects. The vets knew that Rimadyl and oxycodone could cause liver, kidney or other organ problems. However, they had calculated the risks in order for me to have a good quality of life. I heard that phrase a lot. Quality of life. It meant a lot to me that Mom, Dad, and the doctors had always cared about my wellbeing.

Dr. Steve suggested another treatment. He said cortisone shots would provide longer lasting relief as they would help reduce the inflammation caused by bone rubbing on bone. But it too could cause side effects. I ended up getting shots every 60 days or so, along with the daily oxycodone pill.

I had good days that enabled me to walk with Dad while he did his outside chores. I know he liked having me at his side. At times I struggled, but when he noticed my distress he'd say, "Hey big guy, take the day off. Hang out at the house."

Maybe some of the aches were because I was close to eighty in dog years. And like with humans, the calendar doesn't lie. I checked my muzzle in the bedroom mirror for visible signs. There they were. Gray hair, eyebrows, and muzzle. Obvious as spots on a Dalmatian's back.

Dad noticed them too. "Your gray goatee makes you look more mature and dignified. And hey, I have more gray than you do."

**"I am in favor of animal rights as well as human rights.
That is the way of a whole human being."**

Abraham Lincoln

CHAPTER

38

THE INTERMEDIARY

Months later, Tom, who had visited us when he learned of Mom and Dad's divorce, and his wife Cheryl, were celebrating their wedding anniversary in Monterey, California. They invited family, Dad and other friends to join them.

I sat at Dad's side while he petted me and told Mom of his invitation. She encouraged him to go. She said she'd check on Grandma at the nursing home, and of course take care of me. Dad went.

As it turned out Helga, who also had visited Dad in Medford, was the only other person who showed up. Tom said that the other people couldn't make the trip. It all sounded suspicious to me. I mean wasn't it obvious what Tom was trying to do? Afterward, Dad told Mom he had a good time visiting his friends and playing golf on a picturesque oceanside course with Tom.

I noticed after Dad returned home that he spent a lot of time on the telephone. Making calls and receiving them. At the other end? Helga. A few weeks later Helga came from her home in Prescott, Arizona to visit Dad.

She had met Grandma when she first visited. But when Helga saw her at the nursing home, she was shocked to see Grandma so confused about everything.

Mom came to the house, and I thought she wanted to visit with me. However, as it turned out, she was going to lunch with Helga. As they left, they were talking about a fancy Greek restaurant with starched white tablecloths and fresh flowers on the tables. Dad and I shared a TV dinner.

I don't know what they talked about. Dad probably, but I forgave them for abandoning me because both brought back a doggy bag. And needless to say they weren't for Dad.

Helga returned to Arizona and prepared for a long-planned visit to see family and friends in Germany. Her Lufthansa flight was scheduled to leave Phoenix's Sky Harbor airport in early September. On the morning of her trip our phone rang. Even from across the room I heard Helga's excited voice.

"Are you watching the TV? Turn it on!"

Dad ran to the TV. We both saw a plane hit the World Trade Tower. "Oh my God." Dad paced while he talked to Helga. "That's the second plane? Then it wasn't an accident. Some will consider the attack an act of war."

I didn't know what that meant, but I must have had a strange expression on my face because Dad rapped an arm around me. "Don't worry Chase, we're both too old to fight and no one will be shooting at us here."

Helga's trip to Europe ended before it began. So, in a few days she drove up from Arizona in her Grand Cherokee Jeep and brought her dog with her. They were going to stay with us for a few weeks. Misha was a mixed breed with a texture and gold-brown colored fur that were similar to mine,

Maybe I shouldn't tell a lady's age or weight, but Misha was about five years younger than me and tipped the scales at around fifty pounds. Helga thought that she had genes of a German Shepherd, a few from Labrador Retriever stock, and some other breeds too. I thought I saw a little Chow in her.

While I was supposed to be the ridged canine, she actually wore one on her muzzle. She had a six-inch strip of short hair running along the bridge of her nose. Like what I have down my spine. Dad held Misha under one arm and the other around me. He shifted his gaze back and forth. "We must be the only household in Oregon with a pseudo ridgeback and an authentic ridge nose."

Misha stayed close to Helga while in the house, but she also enjoyed the outdoors and the pastures to roam. So we got along okay.

However, we did have one encounter. Dad and I were in the hallway walking toward the master bedroom. And suddenly, snarling, Misha appeared at my side and lunged at my neck. I twisted away as Dad shouted, "No! Stop."

Grabbing her by the nape of her neck, he tossed her, and Misha was airborne for a few feet. She bounced once and turned back toward us. Her fiery glare singed the walls. Dad stared her down, and she retreated into the family room.

Helga had appeared just in time to observe Misha's landing. She heard the racket but had no idea why Dad made an airplane out of her little girl.

Dad looked me over to see if I'd been bitten. Then he took a minute to calm me. When he checked Misha, she quickly rolled on her side, submitting to him. Misha had recovered from earning her pilot's license and the incident left no question that Dad had become the alpha in her chain of command.

"She's okay. No one got hurt," he told Helga, her face a rosy glow.

Steaming that Dad played the Wright Brothers with her baby, she hugged Misha. And Misha wanted to lick Dad's face. "I had to separate the dogs before one got hurt."

I took off for the bedroom while the humans' voices reverberated throughout the house.

I sat on my bed, alert for the 911 call. Then silence. Too silent. I must have looked like honey oozing from a bottle as I slowly tip-pawed toward them.

"Okay, I understand. You were right." I heard her say. They hugged. Misha stood at their feet, wagging her tail. They ignored me as I sauntered up and sat on Dad's foot.

***

I have a tidbit to tell about Misha. In a short sprint, I think she was the quickest of all the dogs that had lived with us. When our original canine clan of guys and gals had played outside, it involved short playful chases or a few darting steps here and there. Compared to them I ran in mud, but it didn't matter to me because we had fun.

With Gabe and the Border Collies gone, the peacocks wandered back to our pastures. Over time they had learned who was fleet of foot and most likely to chase them. As I said, Misha and I were the same color and I think when the birds saw a gold-brown coat appear out of the trees, they probably thought, "Here comes the glacier. Be ready to move out in about an hour."

Well, a few lost some tail feathers before the birds realized I had a smaller clone. They learned to check for size, because there's a huge difference between a glacier and an avalanche.

I found out later that the peacocks came to a sad ending. Dad said that some people didn't like their trademark poop that they often left behind. And I had heard gunshots from across the valley now and then, so I guess some humans couldn't tolerate their occasional messes in spite of the unique beauty they displayed. But shouldn't the punishment fit the crime?

> **"A dog is the only thing on earth that loves you**
> **more than you love yourself."**
>
> Josh Billings

CHAPTER

39

ARIZONA AGAIN

It had been about four years since the divorce, and Dad now was considering returning to Arizona to be with Helga. She had an asthma condition, and she felt much better living in the dry climate than in Oregon's humid weather.

One day in June while Helga went shopping, Dad and I visited Grandma. Afterward we dropped in on Mom. They started talking about Helga, and I saw Mom place her hand on Dad's arm. "Go. Start a new life with her. And don't worry, I'll watch over your mother. And Laura is settled in her apartment near the university. She'll be around to help too."

Laura, now married, had little boy named Lake. They visited often and everyone loved him. Dad played with him a lot, and I know he'll miss the little guy when we move to Arizona. Of course, he'll miss Mom and Laura too.

When we returned home, Helga met us at the door, and Dad said, "We're moving to Prescott." Helga beamed and wrapped her arms around him.

Maybe this is the time to put an end to the tales of my past as

I've reached current day, and I've more or less told you most of my life's journey. There are a few more stories I could add to my memoir, but they are more about Dad' adjustment from a big city banker to a rural farmer.

Like when he'd struggle to get the irrigation water pump working when our weekly allocation was flowing. He did it with words that I'm sure Mom nor Grandma never had heard. Or, the comical times, for spectators, when he tried to clear clogged sprinkler heads on the irrigation pipes. Have you ever showered in muddy irrigation water? Then the times with issues about the septic tank and with our drainage field. And of course, the problems when the well water pump had to be replaced.

But being a quick learner (?), he posted the names and numbers of all the repair people near the phone.

Dad had received the Griffin Creek property as part of the divorce settlement. And Paul, a neighbor, said he wanted to buy it when Dad was ready to sell. On a sunny July morning Paul, Dad, and I stood at the fence near the Shelties' graves to negotiate a price for the mini farm. The spirits of Dancer and Diamond must have been at work because the humans settled on a price in just a few minutes. They both petted me and asked me to witness their handshake agreement.

Dad said I deserved a commission, and when we went into the house, I got two large biscuits. Not bad for a few seconds of work on my part.

Grandma no longer recognized family or friends and Dad could do no more for her. Nor could anyone else. She would be living in the nursing home for the rest of her life. Dad signed the papers that would give Mom the authority to deal with all issues relating to Grandma's care in his absence.

Looking back at my varied experiences on our Oregon farm and as a young dog rescued from the humane society, I've had my ups and downs. They were the good and bad, funny and sad, but always with Mom and Dad at my side and sharing their love with me.

I've lived a great life.

And now as a short timer, I'm preparing for my last journey.

When Mom came by for one last visit around the farm with Dad and me, they briefly discussed me staying with Mom. They worried about how my hips would handle the hilly land around the Prescott house. But remaining in Oregon was out of the question, not only because Mom had a two-story condo, but Dad made it clear he wasn't going to leave me. And I wanted to be with him no matter what.

Dad had the household items that we weren't taking with us auctioned and donated the leftovers to charity. The keeper stuff got loaded into a moving van and it headed for Arizona. Prescott would be our new hometown.

By now the Subaru was about nine years old, and Dad sold it to a friend. He bought a new, blue Toyota Camry sedan to replace it. With everything wrapped up in Medford, Dad helped me onto the back seat of the new car. Misha jumped into Helga's Jeep Cherokee, and in late September, our two-car caravan headed for the great Southwest.

The trip to Arizona was more than one thousand miles, and it took two days to drive there. Helga and Dad stopped regularly to let Misha and me pee and stretch our legs, so we slowed them a bit. We were spending our one night on the road at a place called Bakersfield. When Dad told me the name, my mouth watered. So when we arrived, I expected to see fields of cookies and cakes. Not cotton and corn.

Dad and I had a lot of time to talk on the drive to Arizona. He asked me if I thought he did the right thing by leaving his mother behind. More than once. And I tried, with the most sincere expression I could conjure, to confirm that I thought it was.

I was born in Phoenix but had never been to Prescott, so Dad described it. Nothing like Phoenix. No desert. No palm trees. Not as hot. We would be living outside the city in the mountains and surrounded by tall pine trees. We'd have more snow than in Oregon, and I'd have a lot of fun with new animal smells like javelina. "You know," he said, "We watched them on the Animal Planet, chasing coyotes. They look like wild pigs with tusks. You could play with them."

Dad glanced at me in the rearview mirror and saw me wrinkle my forehead at the thought of javelina as playmates. "Just kidding," he said. "You don't want to mess with those creatures. They're very dangerous."

"We'll be right next to the Prescott National Forest and have a lot of room to roam." I noticed how he looked at me when he said that. We both knew that my exploring days were over.

**"There is no faith which has never yet been broken,
except that of a truly faithful dog."**

Konrad Lorenz

CHAPTER

40

OUR NEW HOME

I liked the house the moment I stepped inside. It had large pictures along the east side that enabled us to enjoy the rising sun and beautiful mountain views. As Dad said, it nestled among huge pines and old dignified oak trees. Outside, a deck wrapped around the northeast side of the house, and I immediately thought of taking sunbaths on a plush rug.

My first morning there, I watched the sun peek over the tree-rich mountains and light up our side of the valley. When I stepped onto the deck, the sunlight made my coat appear as a golden cape, and I felt like an actor walking onto a stage. A cool breeze jostled the trees and created whispering sounds like a litter of puppies swishing their tails.

The deck's east side had a steep stairway of thirteen steps that led to the flagstone patio below. Thirteen was my lucky number. Why lucky? Because Mom had rescued me from cage thirteen at the shelter. But lucky or not, Dad wouldn't let me use those stairs because of my hips.

From the deck I watched the squirrels and chipmunks scurry about for acorns and pine seeds. Some scampered to nearby rock outcroppings and checked out crannies for more goodies. They were so cute. It's funny how aging changes your view of life. A few years ago, I thought of them as snacks but now I see them as nature's critters trying to feed their families.

While I enjoyed being on the deck at any time, the late afternoons were the most pleasant. Especially when the sun slipped behind the western hills and painted irregular shadows all across the valley. At the northern end of the deck a short set of steps led down to a small bedroom-sized dirt plot. It was covered with a chocolate-colored awning and enclosed with a black wrought iron fence. Misha used it as her pee and poop area after it got dark, or on stormy days. I used it too and did my duty while forest smells tickled my nose. By taking a deep breath I would know what critters lurked nearby. When finished I'd struggle back up the steps where Dad always waited for me.

One morning Dad stood by as I headed down. "Stop," he shouted and cut me off before I could continue. "Let's go in the house."

Trouble.

He left me in the kitchen while he hurried to the garage and came back with a long piece of wood. He dashed out to the deck again and in a few minutes he returned.

"Okay, you can come with me now," he said and grabbed a garbage bag from under the sink.

We returned to the deck, and he hustled down to the poop and pee area. While I watched from above, he gingerly placed a snake in the bag.

"A rattler, Chase. I had to kill it. It wouldn't be safe for Misha

162

and you to go down there with it lurking around. And we can't tell Helga about the snake. People would hear her screams all the way to Phoenix."

By that time, even the few steps to and from the potty area was a problem for me. So, Dad built a ramp that covered one side of the steps. That way, depending on how I felt, I could use the ramp or the steps. But finally, we used the front door where there were no steps for me to go out.

A few days after we arrived, Misha saved me from getting into serious trouble. An unfamiliar lady walked into the kitchen from the garage and headed toward me. I kicked into my security role and confronted her with hackles on high.

My growl frightened her, and as I advanced she backed away. Misha saw the developing situation and ran to the woman. She bounced on her hind feet trying to lick the lady's face. A sign of recognition. Thankfully Misha let me know that the lady was friend and not foe. As it turned out, the woman, as she had done for many years, was there to clean the house.

I met Misha's veterinarian the first week after we arrived in Prescott. Helga liked her and thought Dad and I would too. And we did. Dr. Julia checked me out and suggested that I try taking prednisone, a corticosteroid that might help combat the inflammation. We tried it for a while, but after several more office visits went back to the oxycodone.

Each of Dad's discussions with Dr. Julia seemed more solemn than the last. Finally, they concluded that their objective would be to maintain a painless as possible lifestyle for me.

It was early fall and still pretty warm. The snakes were after their last meal and doing some sunbathing before they headed underground for the winter. I know because I saw one. A big one. At our door. Misha dozed at the arcadia door that opened onto the deck when she awoke with an uproar. Dad and I scurried to her side.

"Wow," he said as we saw a large snake slither across the deck, its head already hidden under a large pot next to the door. The tail was still out of sight as it continued up the steps. He knelt beside me as we watched it glide from only a few feet away.

"It's not a rattlesnake because I can tell by the markings on its back. And here comes the tail. It's a gopher snake and it'll keep the rattlers away. It wants to settle around the pot, and we can't have that. Thankfully, Helga's in the shower."

He headed for the garage. I stayed at the door mesmerized by the snake's size.

In a few minutes Dad had guided the snake down the stairs with a push broom. The excitement was over. When he came back he knelt beside me and rubbed my ears. "It had to be at least a five-footer," he said. "I think it's the largest snake I've ever seen."

Misha nestled beside him and licked his face, as if, saying, "my hero."

The first months in Prescott were fun. I guess the excitement of a spacious new home deep in a forest, with magnificent views, helped offset my hip pain. But now my gut ached all the time. I didn't know if I had Ebola, leprosy or another exotic disease I learned about from watching the Science Channel. But you how it is; your thoughts become scrambled eggs when you feel lousy. Being afraid of what you can't see. Like inside a dark, smelly cave.

Dad sensed something other than my hips bothered me,

because he would sit beside me on the floor and gently stroke my back. Of course, I couldn't tell him about my severe stomach pains.

Misha and I got along fine. She understood I wasn't feeling well and left me alone. Ever since Dad pulled her off me in Medford, she had accepted him as the alpha of the family. However, she saw herself as the highest-ranking canine. And she got a little miffed when he focused his attention on me. But whenever Dad took me out, he made sure that she joined us. I enjoyed her company, and besides, Misha showed me all the deer trails around the place. Not that I wouldn't have found them myself, but it was nice not to waste my energy.

To reciprocate, I showed her a few things too. Like how to thump at the dinner table. I still used the technique on Dad, and Misha realized how the leg tap paid off like a busted slot machine. So, Helga got the thump, and the last bite of her food always seemed to disappear into Misha's mouth.

In October Dad flew to Oregon to visit Grandma and he returned in just a few days. His voice cracked when he said she no longer rolled her wheelchair through the halls, but just stayed in bed. When she saw him, her expression said, you look familiar but you've been erased from my memory.

"I was always, no matter what, her little boy who could do no wrong," he uttered. "And now forgettable." Tears trickled down his cheeks when he told me.

The first snow fell later that month. Large fluffy flakes that floated like parachutes. However, Dad didn't plop on his back and make snow angels for me like he did in Oregon. And we didn't have our dodgeball fights. One-sided, of course, because I couldn't throw. Now, they were more of a game of snowball catch. Dad would make a ball and toss it for me to snatch in my mouth.

Now, we only took short walks along the driveway. After a few minutes in the snow I'd be happy to head back to the house and warm my feet.

When Dad visited his mother again right before Christmas, she slept morning, noon, and night. In addition, she refused to eat. I can't imagine anyone not eating, but of course she wasn't well.

He said that many of the caregivers asked about me. I liked that they remembered me.

Christmas came and went. I enjoyed the holidays because I met a lot of Helga's family, and they were all nice to me. Helga made Christmas a special holiday with all the beautiful decorations that she arranged around the house. I liked the seven-foot pine tree with the dozens of dangling salmon-red balls the best. Actually, the balls were more carnation red, but relating them to a food works best for me.

"He is your friend, your partner, your defender, your dog. You are his life, his love, his leader. He will be yours, faithful and true, to the last beat of his heart. You owe it to him to be worthy of such devotion."

Unknown Author

CHAPTER

41

WITH GRANDMA

The following February Dad flew to Oregon again to visit Grandma, and I remember he returned home on a Saturday. The following Tuesday, he got the phone call from Mom. Grandma had died. The news hit me like a swarm of bees jabbing at my stomach.

Grandma loved me and treated me like a human. I remember how in Oregon she would rub my back until her arms got tired. When I could no longer climb onto her sofa to nap she placed a blanket on floor for me. She constantly bragged about me being so smart and how I understood everything she said. Well, who couldn't understand her words of kindness and love?

Maybe it was because of Grandma's passing but I felt weaker than ever. When I had to relieve myself, I would struggle to my feet and stand at the door. Then I kept losing control of my bladder and bowels in the house.

Misha seemed to know when I had to go before I did. I know a lot of canines have a special trait that enables them to detect diseases in humans. And I guess some can sense illnesses in their peers too. She would run to Dad when I messed up and do a little jig to get his attention. I thought Misha was squealing on me but it was actually her call for help.

Dad didn't get it at first, but when the light clicked on for him, he said, "You guys are amazing. Absolutely amazing!" Misha's actions made Helga proud of her and so was I. She was caring for her big brother.

Yet, in spite of her alertness, putrid brown messes like volcanic islands spotted the carpeting

***

I soiled the living room carpet again. I tried to tell Dad that I couldn't help it, and he understood. He didn't say a word and started massaging my hips. My innards now screamed. I tried to stand but my legs didn't have the strength. Like a marionette with all my strings slashed.

Dad watched me struggle and his face turned white. His eyes watered. I never saw him look like that before. He cleaned the accident and snatched a couple of old sheets from the linen closet. He dropped one at my side then rushed to the garage and covered the rear seat of his Toyota with the other. Then he moved the car near the front door.

Helga had gone grocery shopping, and Dad had to cope with me by himself. Kneeling at my side, he carefully slid me onto the sheet, then half-carried and half-slid me across the floor and to the car.

Dad tried to place me on the back seat, but I slid onto the floor like a Slinky down a step. Our eyes met, and I could see his were clouded with tears. From my sprawled position there was no way he could lift me, so he made me as comfortable as he could.

On the way to the vet, it happened again. I couldn't help it. A terrible smelling liquid escaped from my body and soaked the Toyota's carpet. Dad couldn't see me but by the horrible odor, he knew.

My feelings were a jumble. I wanted the pain to be over. Forever. Yet, not before Dad hugged me one more time. I hoped that if I was reincarnated, I'd come back not as a human, but as another dog. And be with Dad.

At the animal hospital, with the help of one of the staff, Dad positioned me on a blanket and the two of them carried me stretcher-like into an examination room. They gently placed me on the floor, and the lady ran to get the vet. Dad sat on the floor with me and pulled me into his lap. I didn't have the strength to open my eyes. I smelled poop on his arm.

"Chase, you've been my best friend. I'll never forget you."

He tried to speak, but he choked on his words. Something about how I always had been a good boy, a good friend. Then, he said, "Chase, I love you."

Dr. Julia came in, kneeled beside us and gently probed my stomach. Each place she touched, I winced. "It's happened," she said. "His kidneys have stopped functioning." She rubbed my ears. "We can't help him."

I remember Dad's loud sob. He mumbled something about his mom. And mentioned my name. His tears dripped on my head as he hugged me tighter. A needle entered my forearm.

Then, I saw Grandma. Reaching for me. A dog biscuit in her hand. I remem. . .

"Having a dog will bless you with many of the happiest days
of your life, and one of the worst."

Unknown Author

CHAPTER

42

MY CHASE

By Dad

Dogs had been part of our family for decades before Chase became a member. For thirteen fun-filled years, the hound sauntered by my side. And during that time, he taught me more about respecting other creatures than I taught him how to coexist with humans.

I enjoyed our time together, lounging on the grass in our front yard or sitting on a bale of hay. I'd talk to him like I would a human. Asked if he slept well. How was he getting along with the other dogs? Once, I even apologized for having him neutered, but explained why it was necessary.

Chase listened and watched me for a word, tone of voice, or body movement that he recognized. And he understood my mood swings long before I appreciated his expressive mannerisms.

We know that fruitful communication between humans requires hearing the spoken word, listening for their intent, and observing the speakers' body language. Most people know that canines communicate their feelings that include anger, fear, and enthusiasm through a wide range of growls and barks. They also send visible messages with their tails, ears, and hackles. And of course, they display their preferences such as where they like to sleep, favorite toy or even desired foods.

So, basic communication between canines and humans does exist. However, if people employ more vigilant observation, a second level of "conversing" with their dogs is likely. Determining the function of a dog's breed–is it a herding dog, a hunter, a terrier or one of the many other dog groups–opens many eyes. So, knowing the purpose of your dog's breeding is a good starting point for recognizing your its wants and needs. If your friend is a mutt, more observation is needed to understand its personality.

Because Chase stayed at my side during most of his years, I was able to observe his mannerisms more carefully than I had with our other dogs. But only when I more conscientiously observed his gait, facial and eye expressions and listened to the tone of his barks, was I able to grasp the promise of a broader two-way communication.

By paying closer attention to Chase and respecting his wants and needs, I believe his life became more satisfying and enjoyable. Yet, in retrospect, I was too slow and inattentive to apply my observation and "listening" skills as soon as I could have.

I believe if dog owners established a routine of reading their dog's mannerisms, they would over time be rewarded with a more meaningful relationship.

Practicing the same awareness with other creatures of nature also could be rewarding. At the bird feeder dangling outside my office window, I see how the morning light illuminates woodpeckers' red halos like an iridescent sun, and how sparrows spit seed hulls like cowboys showering spittoons. Adding to the scene are the jittery chipmunks who park under the feeder, their paws holding fallen sunflower seeds as if in prayer.

Chase was cremated and his ashes placed in an urn. Eyes glistened as we buried him under a huge cedar tree near our Prescott mountainside home. Several days later I spotted a rock the size and shape of a dog's head. It was a remarkable, eerie profile of a long nose, highlighted eyes, and a floppy ear.

Why or how it caught my eye, who knows? Now it serves as a headstone at Chase's grave site. The bank that I retired from was, of course, Chase-JP Morgan. Their branches promote his name and serve as a constant reminder of him, not that he will ever be forgotten. As a fan of the Arizona Diamondback baseball team, I enjoyed going to the ballpark at that time named Chase Park.

In my office there is a framed picture of Chase sitting with me crouched next to him. He has a contented expression on his face and his right paw is draped over my right wrist.

"Once you have had a wonderful dog, a life without one,
is a life diminished."

Dean Koontz

EPILOGUE

BY MOM

Never did I dream that the cute little puppy I carried home from the Arizona Humane Society would become a permanent member of our family and have such an impact on our lives. The Sunshine School for Dogs "experiment" fell apart as soon as I cradled our little guy in my arms, trying to nurse him back to health from his devastating puppy illnesses. (I took some pictures of Chase when he looked like a skeleton, kept the roll in my bag for months and then threw it out. I couldn't bear to see him in his pathetic condition.) The bond that forms as you try to breathe and pray life back into a desperately ill youngster of any species is enduring and immutable.

Except for our first mutt, a hard-to-imagine poodle/dachshund mix, all of our dogs had been sheepherders. I love them for their intelligence and their intense desire to please. And I confess that, in teaching obedience classes, I would snicker from time to time about the seemingly slow progress the hounds would make. Obviously, their handlers did not work between class sessions.

Chase would prove to be a lesson in humility for me. Through him I learned that herding dogs, with their pulsing intelligence and drive, are a slam-dunk for a dog trainer: these dogs can't jump to it fast enough in their passion to please you. But there always seems to be more to it than pleasing the handler; I think it's their over-the-top compulsion to be doing more of the things they love–herding sheep, chasing a ball or Frisbee, running an agility course that makes them react so quickly that they appear to run on batteries. To a hound, however, training (especially obedience training) is a chore. When I would work with Chase, he would hesitate with every command, as if he were evaluating the exercise and trying to see the sense in it. As we practiced heeling, I would stop and then ask him to sit. He would look at me with questioning eyes and then, after a few moments and my cheerful insistence, he would maneuver his large body into a sit. There. I did it. But when I would immediately ask him to heel again, he would look at me with his classic wrinkled brow and really balk this time, as if to say, "Look, Mom, I sat when you asked, but now you're asking me to get right up and start walking again. This just doesn't make sense. What exactly is the point?" I must admit I would have a hard time answering that question.

Through Chase I learned that other types of dogs are at least as intelligent as the herders. But their attitude faces 180 degrees in the opposite direction. The hounds are more independent in their thinking, not relying so much on games and outside stimulation for their satisfaction. The herders seldom want just to sit and be with their person, no questions asked, no activity required. The BCs tolerate their kennel life because, generally, the promise of more activity in the coming day is their reason for living. On the other hand I believe Chase would have withered and died if he had had to live without human companionship.

Much as I love and admire the herding dogs for their breathtaking, almost mystical ability to work livestock, I came to love Chase for simply being who he was. Chase. A dog. A dog who lived each moment of his life as it unfolded. He ran his life the way I have been trying to run mine for years now. He lived in the present. One of the spiritual principles I have been trying to incorporate into my life is the ability to experience each day as it comes, not mulling over the past or fretting about the future.

The herders, I always felt (especially as I look back now), had specific agendas: I need to get Mom to drive me to the sheep. I want to work the sheep. I'd like to work the woollies the way I want if I can get away with it. How can I get Mom to play ball or stick or Frisbee?

But Chase didn't think that way. He just wanted to be with his humans. He exuded unconditional love for us, unconditional acceptance, and apparent gratitude for the comforts of his life. It was Chase's attitude that inspired me to slow down, to take time for reverie and contemplation, for inhaling the essence of the moment. Although I had been moving in that direction for years, it took a mixed-breed, throwaway dog to model this behavior for me.

Now, all these years after Chase was born, I have had many dogs: my last Border Collies and three purebred Ridgebacks. They all adapted well to city life–instead of herding sheep or pursuing lions–they were happy hiking, camping, playing ball at the dog park, and lounging around the house.

The Ridgebacks were especially dear, sweet dogs. Like Chase, they displayed unlimited love and affection. All of us could just sit together, living in the present and enjoying every day of our lives.

"It is man's sympathy with all creatures that first makes him truly a man. Until he extends his circle of compassion to all living things, man will not himself find peace."

Albert Schweitzer

THE END

ABOUT THE AUTHOR

Richard Boich has previously written two novels: a thriller, **The Immaculate Deception,** and a mystery, **The Epitome of Greed and Evil.** He also adapted the *Immaculate Deception* into a screenplay. His other works include the screenplay, *Runaway*.

He is a retired banker who now lives in Northern Arizona.

Made in the USA
Middletown, DE
28 May 2024

54832460R00106